# The Secret
## to
# Incentive Program Success

*Incentive ROI that makes bean counters smile!*

Robert S. Dawson, CITE™
with
Roger S. Peterson, PCM™

ISBN: 1-4392-1509-X
ISBN-13: 9781439215098

# TABLE OF CONTENTS

# DEDICATION

The incentive and motivation industry is changing. It's a change that will affect forever the way incentive programs are planned and implemented. This book reflects the change and why it is needed.

We dedicate this book to those individuals, both incentive buyers and sellers, who have already embraced this change. They know they must deliver a true value proposition to the program participants who must now change how they work to earn incentive awards in the future.

# ACKNOWLEDGEMENTS

Many people have helped to create the process that is outlined here. Some of those people had no idea they were contributing to what I truly believe is a major change for an entire industry, while others were eager to play a part in all of this.

To all you managers, team leaders, line workers and C-level executives who allowed me to probe, ask questions, ask them again, and then allowed me to lecture you on why the awards are not the most important topic for discussion, thank you.

Being able to have this story to tell was not easy either. It all started when I read a brief article in the *Sacramento Business Journal* that mentioned Roger S. Peterson. We became fast friends. After many Starbuck's coffee sessions, Roger finally convinced me that this is a story that needs to be told. Without Roger's encouragement, knowledge, and willingness to be patient with me as I struggled to fit this book into my day, this book would never have happened. It always would have been one of those "I wish I wrote that book" things for me. I am extremely grateful for having met Roger. He is more than a co-author to me. I look forward to our next book (I hope you do, too) soon.

Many of the stories in this book I have used over the years, either in formal workshops, seminars, or in casual settings with friends and colleagues. When this book finally started to take shape, I reached out to many of those same people, those who have heard the gospel preached before and some who have lived the story that is in this book. I want to thank this fine group of people who took the time to read through the manuscript and provide me with some great insights. Bruce Bolger, Mark Repkin, Karen Renk, and Mark Peterman are all involved directly in the incentive industry. Their input was extremely valuable to me. They have a front line view of how they see this ROI process playing a role in the incentive industry. Hal Johnson and Eric Palmaer are two local business leaders whom I admire and respect tremendously. Dan Carmichael and Ted Haus lived through this process with me in the early days. Joe Laipple, an accomplished author himself, provided insights and encouragement that I will always appreciate. Bill Connelly provided a great case study. I very much appreciate having their thoughts and recollections.

# Guest Preface

The time has come for Robert S. Dawson's "The Secret to Incentive Program Success ," and few people are more qualified to produce this work. Dawson has spent the better part of his career pursuing a thankless task: promoting the concept that organizations should apply scientific principles to incentive program design and measurement.

Dawson's challenge is that, for all of the talk of program measurement, relatively few corporations or even incentive companies apply the latest scientific principles to their programs. It's no surprise, given that the subject is hardly addressed in any marketing or management textbooks used in undergraduate or graduate business programs.

Another problem is that many of the people who believe in incentive programs and who regularly use them in their organizations often do so more out of faith and a desire to create an exciting workplace than out of a serious respect for the ability of incentive programs to create an enduring performance – an objectives-based organization. In many other companies, incentives are often a quick fix, do-this, get-that proposition—the old carrot approach.

Dawson's book gives these programs the respect they are due. In a time when organizations seek to build more meaningful relationships with key people and strive to increase market share and sales by keeping customers and by promoting referrals, incentive programs deserve this level of understanding. Drawing on his years of front-line experience with companies seeking a more formal approach to their incentive program design, Dawson combines insight and real-life examples essential to any marketer or manager serious about getting measurable results.

Bruce Bolger
CEO
Selling Communications, Inc.

# Preface

## Is this you…or will it be?

## Why you might want to read this book

Are you in charge of an incentive program? Or will you be? Kind of exciting, right?

Here's the reality: You could be heading into deep trouble. Let's visit a Silicon Valley software company to see what I mean.

If you are a sales executive, you will find this story quite uncomfortable. But face it you must. This company's sales vice president found out the hard way that designing rules with short-term eyes would not deliver the vision of a brighter future.

His company was on a fast growth track, as were many in this high technology wonderland. As is often the case, sales in this company was a competitive sport more than a profession. The sales vice president had his sights on the CEO job. He figured his pathway would be paved by creating sales that would earn the attention of the board.

I reviewed his plans for an upcoming incentive program and had a few questions. "I see you have some aggressive sales goals," I observed. "Your program rules are centered on your sales team qualifying by bringing in new customers and selling more products to existing customers." He beamed. "That's it," he said with a confident slap on the table. "I make our sales team hungry for new business. I set high goals that I know they can reach," he added.

It was a shame to burst his bubble, but my task was to steer the company into an incentive ROI program. So I asked if he had ever gone back and reviewed the sales from previous incentive programs to see how those accounts had performed as customers. "Companies are built on sales growth. Our job as a sales team is to bring in those sales," he asserted. "That's all I look at … new opportunities for sales growth."

After hearing his responses, I knew this guy was not going to be sales boss for long. He was creating a rules structure that he naively assumed everybody – his staff and his superiors – would want. But his rules were destined to create big problems for the business cycle.

His sales team was sharp and aggressive. They enjoyed being challenged to bring in more sales and many of them did actually that. So you can only imagine how they must have felt just 18 months later when the company announced it was laying off a substantial amount of people, including sales staff. Within 26 months, the company completely disappeared from the landscape.

Why? They ran out of cash. Funding became tougher to get as the bubble burst in the valley. The sales vice president called me just before the firm failed. He wanted to know if I had any leads on a new position for him. Over an understandably quiet lunch, I asked, "Did you learn anything from this experience?" Unfortunately, his answer was unproductive. "Yeah, go to work for a bigger company that can afford to stay in business." I offered no referral, but I had to remind him that he actually had the chance to create both additional sales and cash flow for his company.

# Introduction

If you are involved with incentive program planning and implementation for your company, or you are an incentive industry professional who provides that service to your customers, you have just taken the first step to change your incentive program thinking.

Forever.

As you browse through this book, the first thing you will notice is the discussion of incentive awards is delayed until Chapter Ten. That postponement is the foundation of this book and the process for creating a true incentive return on investment (ROI). The awards come *after* you have properly planned your program.

Each chapter will take you through the various steps, with each step supported by real customer stories- *both failures and successes.* One case study runs throughout the book and shows how that company attained real incentive program ROI.

The concepts and methods that are described in this book are not theories. And they surely are not guessing. Guessing has been the engine of incentive programs for years, and that engine is old technology.

These methods are based on science. Independent research has proven that incentives work, as you will see. These are concepts and methods that have been successfully implemented in companies of all industries and sizes. I've made that claim in numerous presentations to many business leaders throughout the years.

But I always run into the same question: "My business is unique. How do I know this will work in my business?" My reply is simple. "It is not a question of *if* this will work in your business, but rather *how well* it will work."

The incentive ROI process outlined here will help transform your management of incentive programs. I consider this concept the most under-utilized, yet potentially most valuable management tool available to managers today.

## My days in commercial banking: Where it all started

In the 1970s, I was a commercial lending officer for a major Boston bank. I dealt with a wide variety of businesses, from Fortune 100 to local entrepreneurs starting new businesses. Numbers and intuition were my tools.

A banker is an interesting position. A banker can obtain cash resources for customers and help them grow and prosper. But from the bank's perspective, a banker's job, in addition to growing and maintaining a customer base, is to protect bank assets.

During my banker days, I also taught at a local community college. The course was for aspiring entrepreneurs eager to have a business of their own. I led these students through reviews of actual anonymous company financial statements. But I soon realized that I was getting a lot of "deer in the headlights" looks from my audience.

Not wanting to cheat any student out of the total experience, I surveyed the group at mid-semester to see if I was reaching my audience. The survey results were revealing. What I learned has become, many years and a whole new career later, the basis for a return on investment (ROI) model that I developed and is now outlined in this book.

My survey indicated my students were lost in all the numbers. We were reviewing companies that had millions of dollars in revenues and expenses. As financial statements changed, we had to re-calculate ratios, changes in cash flow, and so on. And, no, we did not have computerized spreadsheet programs in the early 1970s.

I was simply over the heads of a majority of the class. So I returned to a basic approach that I learned years before. Forget the zeros and commas; they mean nothing in the end. Look at what a change in sales of $1.00 means to a business. Using this format, I took the students through case after case – real companies that I was reviewing – to see if they, as bankers, should lend money to this customer. What became obvious to the students and to me was that these companies were asking for loans to fund sales growth. Therein lies the problem, for bankers and for incentive program managers.

## It's not all about the top lines and bottom lines

As a banker, I always liked to see continued sales growth. The same is true of Wall Street. We all look at the top line first, then the bottom line next and, if that is all good, we're happy. The problem is the lines in between. They can eat away at both the top and bottom line numbers.

Usually such problems don't happen overnight, but over time. Like any slowly developing disease, this disintegration will fester unless you begin to address it along the way. That's what I had my class examine.

We began to study the influence that a $1.00 sales increase has on a business. Using this method, we tracked the impact on this growth to other areas of the income statement, the balance sheet, and the cash flow statement. What we found was something most business executives and owners don't realize because they don't review numbers as often as they should: an increase in sales prompts an increase in capital to support sales. Simple math.

Some students said, as did my banking customers, that banks exist to loan funds for sales growth. That is true to some extent. But at some point the banker must look closely at the business being funded to protect bank assets. As I told my students, it's not easy to tell a customer that no additional funding is available.

Why would I say no? Such a rejection can jump out of the financial indicators of how the company actually manages the capital, such as accounts receivable, inventory, customer support, and direct sales expenses. If receivables are slow, all the bank is doing is temporarily floating the company until its customers pay their invoices. Slow moving inventory is costly, as is the cost of additional staff that exceeds your ability to pay them. At that point, the bank has more of a financial risk in the business than the business owners do, and that puts bank assets at risk. When my banking customers reached this fork in the road, it was time to redirect them from sales growth to better management of the sales they already had.

### Can you take this book to the bank?

No, this book is not about how to borrow money better. It could help you to get better financing terms and financing rates, and it may even help you to reduce your need for funding by showing you how to gather the right financial data.

But this book is about establishing a new mindset. Incentive motivation is not about trips, toaster ovens, TV sets and gift cards. It is not about any awards that you may have received as a participant in an incentive program or awards that your company may have spent good money on in the past.

Rather, incentive motivation is about investing. You are investing in something that can provide your company with the lowest risk and bring your company the highest return of any business investment you can make.

Let me clear up a point: Incentive programs and employee recognition programs are not identical. Incentive programs are designed to prompt change. Participants are told ahead of time, "Do that and you can earn this." Recognition is about an effort or activity that has already taken place. Recognition awards do not involve a carrot put out in front. This book will address incentive motivation only.

> *Let me clear up a point:*
> *Incentive programs and employee*
> *recognition programs are not identical.*

### Then I went from banker to retail travel agency owner

Eventually I left the banking industry and bought a retail travel company. After several years I became familiar with a specialty called incentive travel. It seemed to fit my business background best. The simple overview I learned about incentive travel was that it is used to create incremental sales. Those incremental sales create incremental profits and a small percentage of those incremental profits are used to fund awards for the "winners" of the incentive program. Simple enough, and so I ventured into the world of incentive travel.

Budgets for incentive programs, whether the awards are travel, merchandise, gift cards, or certificates, are created to provide an award experience that will prompt the winning group to keep coming back for more. During good economic times, these programs are funded well because we all love to generate more sales. Motivated sales people will certainly do that. I refer to sales incentives here because, in 20 years in the motivation industry, I've found that 90% of incentive programs are aimed at increasing sales.

While incentive budgets are easier to obtain during good times, they are quickly scrutinized during slow times. Yet companies are hesitant to completely cut these budgets, so the funding sources become interesting, at best, and often downright crazy.

Regardless of what the economy is doing, incentive budgets are usually prepared incorrectly. Budgets that are created on a "what we can afford to spend" or "how much we are willing to pay" basis are really off base. Incentive program budgets should be created as an investment and, as such, they should be given the same due diligence of any other company investment.

Over the years I have witnessed many situations in which incentive program expectations fell short due to a budget cut. That's because nobody told the salesperson. That's the one poor guy who is trudging through ankle deep snow in the middle of winter in Des Moines just so he can reach the incentive quota and enjoy the great program you set up to motivate him. When he arrives on the trip destination, he reacts much like the person who bought a piece of land from an Internet ad. The pictures looked great, but the real experience isn't living up to the pictures. Why? The budget wouldn't allow it!

The budgeting process outlined in Chapter Seven will help you better understand the difference this can make for both your incentive program participants and those employees at company headquarters who support that program.

## Art and science of incentive motivation

As an incentive buyer or provider, you quickly realize the incentive industry can be a great life. After all, the whole emphasis is about creating a positive message and then finding an award that will generate excitement for the participants. Just the shopping experience alone, especially in the incentive travel space, is enough to make most people drool. But like most good things, a price must to be paid and incentives are no different.

The essential question: How do you create an incentive system that (a) improves organization-wide performance and (b) pays for itself? That question has led to a science of incentives. To gain support for your incentive program, you will need to be able to demonstrate true value. True value can involve many things; those factors are addressed throughout the book. Please note the research cited in chapters end notes.

## Defining incentive program ROI

ROI is a term now getting lots of attention in the incentive industry. If you ask for a definition, however, you're likely to get many different answers.

My definition is clear cut and is one that provides a true picture of incentive program ROI: Incentive program ROI is created by incrementally improving revenue and by accounting for all incremental operating costs plus the cost of the incentive program itself. This is the only true measure of ROI for incentive programs. Each chapter adds more clarity and common sense to this definition.

## Why write a book about all this?

Although I enjoy sales and marketing, I have always struggled with my 10 second "elevator pitch." When people ask what I do, I give them a 30 second answer about working with companies to create a return on investment using incentive motivation to improve their business processes. Whenever I get that out, I never hear "Oh, I've heard of that." More often I hear "Huh?"

Understanding incentives is tough enough. But when you add the issue of ROI, the two just don't seem to connect in people's minds.

Many years ago, at a meeting of Silicon Valley executives, I had to explain what it is that I do. Lucky for me, they gave me five minutes, not 30 seconds. After my five minutes were up, one CEO probed me for at least ten minutes more. Judging from their reactions to my responses, I had indeed created a unique niche in the incentive industry. The niche was surely something executives would love to understand and embrace.

But most executives don't really do it right because it sounds, well, too "financial." I continued my responses with some brief examples – war stories – of what this method has done and can do for companies. At that point, one of the CEOs summed it up by observing, "It sounds like what you have is like a cure for cancer, but you can only help those who are willing to have the treatments."

I could not have said it better myself.

I have written this book in the hope that I can reach at least a few sickly incentive patients who will learn and benefit from a positive treatment for what may be ailing their business. I do know this. If you stay the course with what is outlined here, your business will emerge much healthier than those who pick this book up and then put it back on the shelf.

It's decision time. Are you putting this back on the shelf or are you ready to change?

Robert S. Dawson
Founder
The Business Group
www.businessgroupinc.com

# Chapter 1:

## Compensation: Building an incentive program on solid ground

> *"Most Americans say they want more money. Yet non-cash awards appear to be more effective motivators."*
>
> — Jerry McAdams,
> **Maritz Information Resources**

### An essential starting point

We start first with the issue of compensation because it is important for building what I call your incentive foundation. If you don't tackle this subject first, your incentive programs will wobble on shaky ground.

Incentive programs are not always aimed at employees. You might aim an incentive program at dealers, value-added resellers, independent sales representatives, distributors, or other non-employees. Experiences with such incentive target audience are included throughout this book. You will soon begin reading a serial case study involving both internal sales employees and independent distributors.

Regardless, never forget that your own employees play a vital role in your incentive plans. Your employees are involved in making that happen. Don't make the mistake of thinking your employees will not notice or care that your incentive program is affecting their workload for which they receive no award.

### The Gist

Upon reading this chapter, you should feel us reaching out from the covers and shaking you by the shoulders. You should be struck with a new reality: compensation and incentive are separate domains. Avoid confusing them in the minds of employees or you will create a false sense of entitlement – and that's no incentive for new behaviors or actions. If employees see an incentive as an entitlement, like their paycheck or benefits, your incentive program is sunk.

Part of this new realization is that you must view every incentive program – be it for sales, production, safety, or other functions – as an investment in new behaviors, not an expense. You then can build an incentive program with return on investment (ROI) or economic value added (EVA)...an approach that is demonstrated throughout this book.

## Why did they react that way?

How many times have your colleagues or your spouse reviewed possible incentive awards and reacted, "Wow, these are great choices." Instant hits, they predicted. Or, how many times have you headed into a presentation for a new incentive program thinking your award choices would be equally exciting to the targeted participants?

But how many times have your incentive awards prompted the reactions you expected? Instead, you heard reactions such as these:

- "Hey, what's going on? These awards aren't as good as last year's awards!"
- "This resort isn't in the same league as the one we were at last year."
- "I don't need or want anything in this catalog…what were they thinking?"
- "Is this instead of a raise this year?"

Why do you get such surprising reactions? Incentive awards are often offered as a gesture of goodwill, especially when the company recognizes that times are tough for employees. But participants may not see things that way. This clash in perceptions looms larger when day-to-day living costs are increasing. Incentive participants are not immune to these costs. Participants who are new to incentive programs might view a well-intended incentive award as another excessive expense.

But incentive programs are not just about creating goodwill. They are also an opportunity to motivate your employees to achieve above and beyond goals. The awards then should be something they would not or could not buy on their own. When they earn that award, it truly is special. The problem is that incentives have to match the aspirations and the realities of contemporary living.

> *Many sponsoring companies inadvertently blur the lines between incentives and compensation. Even well meaning executives struggle to build an effective incentive program that is not perceived as part of base compensation and benefits.*

## The big differences

Confused? Let's differentiate three important concepts.

**Salary and benefits are base compensation.** An employee is entitled to compensation and benefits as a condition of employment. No confusion there, right?

**Bonus compensation is variable compensation** paid for meeting job requirements, such as closing sales. Any one who deals with sales professionals knows the role of bonuses.

**Incentives should be distinct from any *anticipated* compensation**. An incentive participant earns an award for achieving targeted behaviors and results that are not specified or even mentioned in employment contracts or job descriptions. Incentive programs are about special goals that require special attention…and the fun of achieving such goals.

If an employer is trying to retain good people by paying bonuses just to make up a difference in salary, such an approach will work only temporarily. Employees will eventually dismiss such an incentive bonus as the long-awaited correction to their salary: "That's the compensation I am entitled to."

At that point, employees begin mumbling a cynical question: "So what are you going to do for me now?" Meanwhile, the employer discovers nearly everyone is in the bonus pool, and many or all employees are earning that bonus each time period.

Remember the days when Silicon Valley companies hosted beer parties on campus for all employees? Employers' attorneys became nervous about possible liability issues. But it was hard to take away these weekly festivities. They were expected. Employees felt entitled. "What happened to our weekly kegger?"

## Don't confuse incentive programs with employee recognition programs

Employee recognition programs are constantly mislabeled as incentive programs. A critical difference exists. An incentive program is a carrot held out to achieve some goal or change. Basic behavioral psychology. If you do this, you will get that. Recognition awards are after the fact. You've done a good job. Here is our way of saying thank you.

> ### *The reality:*
> ### *Something that is regular and expected is not special. If it is not special, why work extra for it? Instead of excitement, such an incentive program can actually build resentment.*

### When cash works…and then stops working

I am often asked about using cash as an incentive. Most people assume I am against that because I stress the importance of separating incentives and compensation.

Cash can be and often is used as an incentive. Sometimes cash works, but its workings must be carefully monitored because it can easily become compensation in the minds of program participants. As with any incentive award, you have to be sure that you are creating an incentive with the award, not an entitlement.

Incentive programs are like any other business strategy you employ. Timing is everything. A great example is a large marketing fulfillment and distribution company I once worked with. The CEO was adamant that only cash could be used for incentives. The CEO introduced a cash bonus program to motivate the employees to be a part of the company's success. But it's important to note that the company's base compensation was about 30% below market wages

Here's how the program rolled out. Each of six distribution centers was turned into its own business unit with a separate profit and loss (P&L) statements. At each center, 50% of the profits went into a bonus pool for that site's employees. They became virtual shareholders in their distribution center and, as such, they were allocated internal shares of the bonus pool based on their positions in their distribution center.

The general managers conducted monthly P&L meetings at their distribution centers. The purpose was to explain to floor workers the flow of revenue and expenses into their distribution center. The employees, at a glance, could see how their actions influenced the flow of money. The bonus shares showed them their personal bonus potential at the end of each quarter, which is when bonuses were paid.

I wanted to know first hand if this program was really something that the floor employees fully understood, or were they just looking at the bonus amount and nothing else. One employee summed that up for me rather quickly when I asked him if he understood the business he was in and how they generate money for the company.

"Mr. Dawson, it's really simple," said Miguel, a receiving clerk in one of the centers. "The trucks back up to the loading dock and it's up to us to get the pallets unloaded. We count the materials to make sure we know how much we are receiving to our distribution center on behalf of the client. That's very important. Once we take it in, we own the responsibility to have it all here when they need it sent out to them. We charge the client to do this. Then the right cartons have to be placed in the right client storage area. The client pays for that, too. Then the fulfillment orders come in. We have to make sure the right materials are sent to the right place...all by 5 PM. We charge the client again. If we don't get it out by 5 PM, we lose money because we guarantee that we will ship those orders by 5 PM. We work really hard so that our clients keep sending us their materials for storage and fulfillment. That way we don't have to find new clients each year to replace unhappy ones," Miguel added with authority.

Wow! To my amazement, it appeared that every hourly fulfillment worker had completely understood the dynamics of making a profit by serving the customers...and making a bonus in return. It worked.

But here's the rub. After several quarters of some rather large bonuses, many of the employees began to buy some high-end merchandise, from guitars to motorcycles. In some cases they were spending money *in anticipation of a quarterly bonus.*

Sadly, the once profitable bonus program became a form of compensation. Cash can work as an incentive, but you must monitor its effectiveness. We'll deal with that in Chapters Eight and Eleven.

## What the research says about incentives

Numerous studies have been done about effective incentive and motivation programs. Research is available to substantiate what I've known for years.

We all know that sales professionals love bonuses. One recent study confirmed that 71% of sales respondents believed cash works best as a motivational tool.[1] A sales compensation plan that lacks bonuses for reaching quotas would indeed be an unusual way to motivate sales people.

But one study of how cash bonus recipients spent their check is revealing.[2] Among the 374 surveyed employees who received a cash bonus in 2006, the most common action taken was to pay off debts (36%). The second most mentioned action (28%) was to purchase gifts during the holidays. Investing took 27% while 11% of respondents reduced long-term debt. Another 27% bought consumer products.

But only 8% treated themselves to a big award for reaching their incentive goals. Why?

The explanation is simple. While cash may be king, it can't buy the crown that commands respect. We call it trophy value.

Cash is spent. It disappears. But non-cash incentives have a life span that builds pride and recognition. Such tangible awards remain a reminder to recipients and their colleagues that the company values those employees' performance and employment.

A study of 235 incentive managers provides good insights. Although 60% of the managers used cash incentives, they preferred non-cash programs. Non-cash incentives were seen as "more effective for all of the organizational objectives assessed in the study."[3] Cash incentives were seen as more effective for increasing sales, customer acquisition, and referrals. But non-cash incentives were preferred for customer service personnel and other support staff.

A contradiction here? As you read this book, especially Chapter Six on perceptions, you will see the need to treat each incentive program participant group as unique. Each year is different. The economy and other conditions change. All this affects the attitudes of participants in an incentive program.

What does management think about such attitudes? Another survey indicated that 25% of executives say they don't give awards to recognize top sellers.[4]

Presumably, such executives think the bonus is all that's needed. Maybe they are the managers who naively believe their employees are fully content and truly loyal. Or perhaps they are the managers who dismiss unhappy employees with a "That's the job, take-it-or-leave it" stance.

Who doesn't like being praised and recognized for good work? What these managers are sadly overlooking is the cost of finding, training, and developing a replacement for a lost employee. An investment in incentive programs can greatly cut turnover costs, and a properly designed incentive program can boost performance by 25 to 44%.[5] That's a double return on your incentive investment.

## Introducing our serial case study: A California tool manufacturer

Success stories tell it all. Using my incentive ROI method to design and implement your incentive program can greatly benefit your organization. To illustrate how, I will use throughout this book the story of a long-term client.

This company is a medium-sized Southern California manufacturer of hand tools. The CEO had a great business. The company had been privately held since its inception in the 1970s. Assembly line employees, while highly skilled, were paid an hourly wage.

One day the company CEO, whom I knew through another business affiliation, took me aside. "Hey Bob," he asked, "can you help me put together one of those incentive trips you're always talking about?" My immediate reply was, "Surely. But what is it you want to change with an incentive?"

His chuckle alerted me to what I usually hear during these casual conversations. "I just want to grow our sales," he replied.

Such comments are typical whenever I am asked what kind of work I do. I usually answer something about sales incentives, since that's a familiar concept to business managers who equate incentives with exotic trips and the latest electronics.

But here is the problem: Business managers still have the impression that incentives are something that can be used to push employees when a company needs to push for more specific results, such as improved production.

These managers are constrained by the company compensation plans and don't even know it. They should not implement a bonus or cash award program without first taking other steps – such as an objective critique of compensation.

But more often than not, no such compensation study is done. The result is an incentive program that clashes with the employees' view of what they should be receiving.

Often managers use their department budgets to buy incentive awards that can be expensed as a marketing or promotional cost. Without thinking about the true relationship between compensation and incentive, these well-meaning managers sponsor incentive "contests" or spiffs or use other non-cash incentives they think will drive results. The problem is the participants may see these awards as an alternative to deserved additional compensation: "Why are they trying to give us this award when I really need the cash to buy groceries this week?"

We'll come back to this story shortly, but I want to cover an important concept first.

## Why tangible non-cash awards can work better

One large company wanted to test the relative effectiveness of a cash incentive program versus one offering travel and merchandise awards. The results were remarkable. The non-cash participants increased their sales 46% more than the cash-only group. [6]

An incentive industry executive white paper described further dynamics.[7] Apparently, tangible awards are not confused with base compensation the way a cash bonus goal might be.

A cash award quickly disappears into the bank account. In the participants' minds, their bank account becomes emotionally disconnected from the employer. No lingering trophy value remains to build pride. But tangible non-cash awards, such as pictures of a Bermuda outing or the oak plaque in the office, remain identified with the issuing employer. Forever.

Second, cash has absolute value: A $1,000 bonus check is worth $1,000. Not so with a group trip award for qualifying participants because the dollar value is difficult to assess, especially at group rates. Cash goes into a bank account. Non-cash awards go into an emotional account.

Third, emotions come into play, according to industrial psychologists. If you have earned a berth on the cruise ship to Jamaica, the vision of restful trip keeps building in your mind … good food, walks on the beach, and romantic evenings with your spouse. One thought leads to another.

Fourth, a participant does not have to rationalize the cost of a tangible award that he or she might never personally buy. It's been earned with hard work meeting goals. Enjoy! What's more, the harder the participant worked for the award, the more valuable that award builds in the participant's mind.

Fifth, it's tacky to walk around the office bragging about your cash bonus. But tangible awards are easy to talk about, whether the award is a trip or a season's pass to a sports team. It's easy for colleagues to ask about such awards and its fun to talk about them. And the discussion reminds those colleagues that they, too, might want to strive hard in the next incentive program. It's called trophy value for a reason.

In short, trophy value is added value.

> ***Cash goes into a bank account.***
> ***Non-cash awards go into an emotional account.***

### The California manufacturer faces reality

Let's return to my client, the CEO of the hand tool manufacturer in Southern California. We agreed to meet and explore incentive options that might work for his situation. But as soon as I was escorted to his office, I saw some immediate signs that indicated there were a lot of things to discuss beyond his immediate thoughts about an incentive program.

His office was perched on the second floor of the plant. He looked down on the plant floor where he could watch the daily ebb and flow of his workers. During my visit, I caught several eyes sneaking glances of us as the CEO proudly waved his hands over the plant landscape, almost like a king surveying his domain.

As I continued our discussion, the CEO ventured into the same mindset that most business owners and executives enter: He wanted to make a "statement" with a "prize" that would wow his employees. Then he listed all the ideas he and his wife were certain would be great motivators – the typical trips and high-end merchandise list.

(Note: Sometimes it's the spouse. Sometimes it's the neighbor. CEOs retain attorneys and accountants, but think nothing of asking the wrong people for suggestions of awards to motivate other people. After all, how does the spouse, uninvolved in the business, know what might motivate employees rarely seen?)

I put a lid on his excitement as I moved the conversation away from the "buy mode" to a more strategic process. "Rather than looking at what incentive would attract the attention of your employees," I asked, "let's talk about who they are, what they do, and how much you pay them to do what they do."

His puzzled expression is one I've seen before. He was surely asking himself, "Why does Bob need that information just to buy trips and merchandise? "Bob, I am a good employer," he assured me. "My employees average seven years with me and they love our company. We pay well and have great benefits."

14

While I did not doubt the CEO's firm assertions, I could not build an effective incentive program for his employees without a sound foundation underneath it. "Great, that is something to be proud of," I replied. "But just to be sure we have a solid base, let me survey your employees. Let's ask them what they think about life at the company. As you know, Maslow's Hierarchy of Needs theory comes into play when you introduce incentives into your company."

He had no idea how some guy named Maslow played a role in his company. I briefly explained the famous hierarchy. If you have not reviewed it since you took Psychology 101, I have included it in the appendix of this book. It's practical and makes lots of sense for incentive managers.

Although my client thought this survey would be a waste of time, he allowed me to deploy it with the help of his human resources department. I reached out to one of my many resources, a company that specializes in the design and deployment of employee surveys. Within a couple weeks, we had a survey instrument that was ready to begin. Department meetings were used to announce the survey to all employees. They were told their participation was strictly voluntary and would remain totally confidential.

The survey garnered 78% employee completion. But it also confirmed what I usually see when a company manager or executive attempts to supplement compensation with incentives. The employees believed they were not receiving a fair wage for the work they provided. Many believed the CEO spent money on things that didn't matter instead of providing a better working environment.

This was predictably tough news to break to the boss. But after getting over my refusal to share who said what, he actually took the news fairly well. I suggested he forget about an incentive program and consider a compensation study to determine if the wages and working conditions were competitive. Otherwise, I told him, any incentive would quickly provoke the killer question: "Why doesn't he just give me the cash instead?"

Perhaps you have not actually heard those words from your incentive participants. I can assure you, these comments arise in many incentive programs. Maybe yours. Maybe right now!

I will take you through, in the chapters that follow, how this particular CEO learned to silence that negative message. More importantly, I will show you how he and other CEOs who have used my incentive ROI method to create measurable results.

## Time to change your incentive terminology

The right terminology helps you create an effective program. An incentive program targets goals and behaviors you want the participants to achieve with future action. The participants who earn the award are being recognized for their achievement.

But don't confuse incentive programs targeting future behavior with employee recognition programs that award past behaviors. An employee recognition program provides awards for behaviors in the recent past. An incentive program is about longer-term, more company-wide, improvements. Both are important management tools.

Awards offered in incentive programs are earned because the participants met certain goals. They did not win a prize at some lucky game of chance. Rather, they accomplished something using skill. Thus, using terminology such as contest or winner in an incentive program sends the wrong message.

Such distinctions are important. Unlike anticipated compensation or other entitlements of employment, incentive awards offer participants increased status and convey the notion that successful participants are leaders among their peers. If an employee wins a $1,000 in Las Vegas, he or she is regarded as lucky, but no more than that. If an employee earns an award for meeting an incentive goal, colleagues know full well the award was earned with hard work. They might well consider working just as hard. So your incentive program should avoid such terms as prize, contest, or winner.

### The take-away

**Guiding principle:** Incentive programs are great management tools but, like any management tactic, they need to be used properly to be effective. Consider your compensation plan as the foundation of your business, much like your home is built on a foundation. Once that foundation has been poured, cured and then examined, the builder begins to add the framework to your home.

**Solution:** Incentives are built the same way. Each room of your home is added based on the amount of foundation you have available to support those rooms. Your incentive program can be "built" only if you have that type of foundation for your company.

**Example:** Are your compensation and benefits in line with the norms for your industry, your geographic location, and the job descriptions of your employees? Are they keeping up with an ever-changing world economics? Compensation and benefits are what your employees see as things they *need*. Incentive awards are things they *want*.

## How does your incentive program measure up?

A few simple questions can tell you if your program is heading in the right direction:

- Is your incentive program kept separate from base compensation and benefit programs, including such variable compensation as cash bonuses?

- Do your program awards meet the key test: *"I could not or would not acquire this on my own"*?

- Are you tailoring the awards to the participant so that each participant group is likely to view their award as offering perceived value? A second flat-screen television does not offer perceived value to someone who already owns one. Neither does a trip in the middle of the school year to someone who has no relatives to watch the children.

- Have you surveyed your employees to gain insight into their perceptions about your company compensation plan and overall work environment? Does your compensation plan measure up to Maslow's Hierarchy of Needs for your employees? Is employee training or organizational change needed before an incentive program is implemented?

- Is your incentive program called a contest and are the participants called winners? If so, you are not conveying the sense that participants earn awards for targeted behavior.

Now you are aware how important your compensation foundation is to the success of your incentive program. It is now time to alert you to the importance of how your business activities flow through your organization and its employees.

## End Notes

[1] *Sales & Marketing Management* magazine (2004) Equation Research survey of 335 executives.

[2] Smith, A.E. (2007 April 4). The Principal Financial Group

[3] Peltier, J., Schultz, D., & Block, M. (2005 December 23). Strategic guidelines for managing cash and non-cash employee motivation programs. Forum for People Performance Management and Measurement, Northwestern University.

[4] *Sales & Marketing Management* magazine, ibid

[5] Stolovitch, H. et al (2002, January). Incentives, motivation and workplace performance: Research and best practices. International Society for Performance Improvement and the Incentive Research Foundation (IRF, www.theirf.org), formerly SITE Foundation. White paper based on study available from IRF.

[6] Goodyear Tire & Rubber Company study from the mid-1990s.

[7] Jeffrey, S. (2003). The benefits of tangible non-monetary incentives. Incentive Research Foundation (IRF). Dr. Jeffrey is in the Department of Management Sciences at the University of Waterloo, Ontario, Canada.

# Chapter 2

## Your Business Cycle: Like water running through a garden hose

The toughest part of understanding a return on investment (ROI) strategy for incentive programs is grabbing your attention from buying awards and refocusing it on managing the process your program creates. Even as I write this, such refocusing sounds hard to do. I know all too well that when the word "incentive" comes up, minds automatically jump to the word "award."

Over the years I have had many opportunities to present the ROI method described in this book. I have had audiences consisting of CEOs, CFOs and COOs as well as managers who were directly responsible for planning and implementing incentive programs.

At first, they all wanted incentive programs that were justified with proven ROI. But when they heard what it took to gain ROI, well, the "awards mentality" took over and ROI becomes a second thought.

If I could just show these smart folks the financial impact that an incentive would have on just one aspect of their business, I thought, they would surely understand what an incentive program could do throughout their company. After all, it does not take a Harvard MBA to figure out that if you induce additional activity at one point in a business cycle, such as sales, other areas of the company would feel the effect of that change.

I usually got head nods when I explained that, but with eyes slightly glazed.

Then one day I found an old hose in my garage. As I was walking to the garbage can, the magic moment hit me. I cut off a four-foot piece and threw the rest away.

The garden hose is a common household object. With usage and weathering, hoses develop invisible cracks. By turning up the pressure from the faucet, worn spots worsen or burst. But routine examination of the hose uncovers worn spots so you can take action. The operative words: routine examination.

Imagine the departments of your business as a simple garden hose. Think of incentive programs as water under high pressure running throughout your company. You have to look for places where an incentive program could cause a problem. I carry that hose in my briefcase to make a point that many executives otherwise just don't get. It's called business cycle flow review.

---

**The Gist**

A simple overview of your business cycle, how your company goes to market, can provide your company with a chance to improve both cash flow and profits as a result of your incentive program.

---

### Business cycle review – the incentive garden hose

Incentive programs are intended to produce change and movement. Change has a ripple effect. But executives and managers are often focused on the department targeted for the incentive program. They do not consider the possible impact the program's success might have on their overall business cycle and supply chain.

Studying the elements of your business cycle gives you a 30,000-foot view of how your company goes to market. This vantage point helps to gauge the organization's overall ability to handle additional activity.

Your company's business cycle begins when you purchase resources (e.g. raw materials, personnel, data) and ends when your product or service is sold, fulfilled, and the revenues collected. Your business cycle also includes any after-sales service your company provides, such as installation or customer support. In short, it includes any point of customer contact.

If your business is based on a channel or distribution model, your business cycle is more complex. Many channel distribution models involve businesses that may compete with each other.

The importance of a review of the business cycle and supply chain was discussed in the *Harvard Business Review*.[1] "Supply chain considerations (and expertise) should be core components of business planning, including sales and marketing promotions, and of contract negotiations with customers and partners," the authors assert.

---

*Imagine the departments of your business as a simple garden hose. Think of incentive programs as water under high pressure running throughout your company. You have to look for places where an incentive program could cause a problem.*

For example, the authors caution managers to avoid short-term thinking, such as discounting prices near the end of a quarter. Such repeated actions merely train buyers to wait to quarter's end before purchasing, and that slows sales in the next quarter.

The supply chain, unfortunately, can be relatively invisible to some employees. The HBR authors described how railroad terminal managers were evaluated solely on how many railcars could be moved with each locomotive. The managers did just that, clearing the yards of as many railcars as the engine could pull. But they consistently stalled the movement of shorter trains that carried the payloads of the railroad's most profitable and valuable customers.

Many CEOs experience the shock of production or cash flow issues too late, when a simple review of their business cycle would clearly point that out during the course of everyday business.

Why does this occur? Often times it is a matter of who gets the attention. The supply chain management staff may be jumping up at the meetings to get that attention.

Another way to describe business flow is a business map. "If you can't draw it, you don't understand it," says business researcher Geary Rummler. He and colleagues show how business maps are great tools for understanding your organization and how it really operates.[2]

Incentives work, but make sure they work the way you want. Your marketing and sales staff may be eager to spin a new promotion, but doing so when the production department is retooling or understaffed could result in disappointed customers.

## My great awakening to the pitfalls of incentive programs

I know first hand how critical this process is to the long-term success of your incentive program. When I was a provider of incentive programs for companies, I never thought about this at all.

Then three key clients asked me to operate their incentive program – with approximately 30–40% fewer budget dollars. That budget reduction caught my attention because many other companies were in the midst of tough economics. Cutbacks and layoffs were commonplace. What was I heading into?

But the big surprise came when I asked the management at each company how we could still operate their program on the reduced budget. Here's how all the conversations went.

"Will the group size be smaller?" I asked with optimistic anticipation.

"Ah, no. Same size as last year," came their reply.

"Oh, I see," said I.

"Will the number of days for the trip be fewer?" I asked.

"No, we would like to keep that where it is," was their response.

You get the idea: Do more for less.

As good as I thought my ability could be at helping companies with incentive programs, I could not figure out how I could do *the same program* for 30–40% less. It was this very taste of reality that put me on the path to the ROI incentive method that I now employ.

I was unable to work with these three clients that year. Yes, that was a big revenue loss for me. My relationship with the senior executives at all three firms, fortunately, was on solid ground. They understood why I could not operate their incentive program under such circumstances. Of course, my competitors had no problem with the numbers.

But the loss opened a door that I am now walking you through. I knew what I wanted to uncover was in the long run far more important to both me and the incentive industry as a whole.

I looked closely at why these client companies were in this draconian position. I think the old banker in me started to kick in. Specifically, I examined what was really taking place with the incentive programs I had been designing and implementing for these clients.

It had been hidden in plain sight right in front of me.

We were creating additional sales and increasing revenue, but we were not looking at what such revenue increases had done to other areas of their companies. So, I set out to interview, with everyone's permission, the managers of the departments that would have been impacted by our sales incentive program.

My findings were shocking, even to me.

Financial managers told me stories of "how you and your incentive program caused our accounts receivable to go from 35 to more than 90 days." Operations managers told me they were forced to run another shift due to an increase in volume and the demand for immediate fulfillment. These additional shifts required new hires that were not as skilled as the team they had. That raised concerns about additional safety, production quality, and overall labor cost.

It didn't stop there. Customer service center managers had delays handling incoming calls compounded with complaints about broken promises from sales people, late deliveries and wrong products…the list went on and on.

I gathered this information, feeling lucky that these stressed managers didn't seek revenge on me. I was startled at how much they told me about "what *your* program did to *my* area." They felt so personal about it.

None of these problems and emotions was ever tied back to the incentive program that would surely do what we wanted it to do – increase sales. So I tied the results of the incentive program to the financial data of the various departments that unloaded all these complaints on me.

That led to a scary conclusion: Incentive programs do work, but they can do a lot of harm as well as good.

Sales incentive programs increased revenue, all right. In addition, they produced some real business cycle flow issues.

In the case of one of the clients, sales came in from new accounts. At first, I thought that was a good thing. But the financial managers had another view. Some of these new accounts had shaky credit. Several accounts brought in are still in collections.

I will never forget the one financial manager who showed me the past due list of these accounts, and said, "My understanding is that the sales team got incentive credit for these accounts and those reps went to Hawaii. Now I am fighting hard just to collect these invoices."

Does that have an impact on cash flow? You bet it does!

Not every incentive program I handled caused problems in receivables. Some prompted operational difficulties. Give a sales person an incentive to sell and watch out. I saw, first hand, where sales were being closed even though delivery schedules were nearly impossible to meet. I saw products weighing hundreds of pounds shipped overnight to meet customer demands so the sales person could earn incentive points for that Hawaii trip.

Does that increase operating expenses that force down profits? You bet it does!

The stories go on and on. Can you see how an increase in revenue is not always a perfectly good thing?

## But some still can't see the leaks ... or even the flow

The analogy of the garden hose is used frequently in this book. As I have already pointed out, the garden hose model came to me after many attempts to illustrate the business cycle flow concept. It's an effective demonstration tool, but some managers don't get it.

I recall presenting the incentive ROI concept to the staff of a performance improvement company. I was discussing the importance of business cycle flows and actually had my trusty hose on the table by the projector.

But one senior manager was clearly unimpressed. "I've been doing sales programs for thirty years," he said with absolute confidence. "Never have I heard a client worry about business cycle flow. The sales programs I have done have always been about moving excess inventory. That's why they need an incentive – to move that inventory!"

I smiled and replied, "If that's the case with your clients, fine. Just skip this part of the process if you have already considered any unforeseen problems that might be tripped by a sales incentive program."

What this manager said was revealing. For one thing, it's apparent he did not pay much attention to finding out how his sales incentive programs affected his clients. If the programs produced any negative impacts, he did not know. While I am sure both he and his client were looking solely at the top line, the revenue, I suspect that they were not interested in taking a closer look at what the true cost of sales was. After all, their objective was to sell more "stuff" and that's what they did.

This lack of foresight, especially by a long-time sales executive, is not unusual. He has been focused for too long on selling the "sizzle." I understand the attitude. Before I started to understand what these incentive programs really did, I was just like the thirty-year incentive veteran. I now admit that I was just spending incentive budget funds instead of providing valuable incentive programs that caused positive change throughout a company. My focus was on getting my clients the best bang for their buck, making sure we would "wow" the participants, so they would go out and sell…sell…sell.

Successful incentive programs don't work that way. Today we see companies like Amazon fulfilling incentive awards, so just about any merchandise award is readily available. Trips, whether group or individual, can be easily arranged anywhere a person wants to go. The world has grown smaller.

The days of wowing incentive participants with just awards are over. If your incentive program is not creating added value in the minds of participants, you will never build the "could not, would not buy on their own" mentality. Sadly, such shortcomings are typical with many incentive programs. But by reading this book and considering its implications, you will never fail to see the leaks.

### A short success story…

A manufacturer of flooring materials needed to increase market share. Management was about to launch an incentive program to boost dealer sales. But during a planning session, the operations manager wisely observed that his department would need to increase its skilled labor force and upgrade equipment to handle increased sales volumes. He remembered flat sales years that prompted a downsizing in operations. The incentive meeting came to a cold, stark halt.

One manager bolted to the white board. Other department managers jumped in to add their own details to a rough flow chart of the company's overall business cycle, from the purchase of raw materials to after-sale customer service. The revised flow chart revealed that a plan to increase sales, implemented without considering all aspects of their business cycle flow, *would disrupt several areas of the business.*

The firm's management began improving all points in their business cycle until they were certain they could process additional sales. Only then did they begin what became a successful incentive program for their dealers.

## ... but how one program failed

A beverage distributor launched an incentive program aimed at retailers to increase sales of selected items. The six-month program, based on case quantity purchases, was well received. Orders poured in.

But after three months, managers discovered that the incentive program had overpowered shipping. No one had given operations the chance to prepare adequately for such increased volume. Retailers had run promotional campaigns to help push the product, and now upset customers demanded what ads had promised. What's more, customer service phones were overloaded with retailers' calls for help.

A simple review of the production process would have spotlighted this possibility. In the end, no one was happy…not the distributor, not the retailers, and not their customers.

## Our California manufacturer

Let's continue to use this California tool manufacturer throughout the book to help you follow my incentive ROI process, step by step.

After the CEO revised the company's compensation plan, I returned to discuss the original topic: an incentive program. "OK, Bob, so the compensation plan is fixed…now can we have an incentive program?" my CEO friend asked.

Although he had become wiser about the benefits of incentives, his thinking was still stuck. Our initial conversations will show you what I mean.

"My employees really do like the company, but if you need to do another survey, go right ahead!" he said assuredly. I advised him that, yes, we would still need a baseline survey, but I urged we first start the planning by reviewing his company's business cycle.

"You mean the high and low sales cycles for our business?" he asked. His mind was still fixed on increasing sales.

I replied that we needed to review how his company goes to market, how sales flow through the business, and what departments are touched in that cycle. But that's something CEOs don't want to hear when they are trying to grow sales. So I reached into my briefcase and pulled out that trusty, worn-out garden hose.

The look on his face was priceless, as it usually is when I do this exercise. But my garden hose has proven to be the simplest way to demonstrate the importance of my ROI process.

I started by asking them to pretend that sales (or revenue) would come into the business the way water enters the garden hose at its connection to a faucet. Every time sales (revenue) increases, you are simply turning the faucet to increase the amount of water that goes into the hose. That part he got.

But then I pointed out some worn spots on the hose. The top layer of hose had been worn such that you could see where the water would be flowing. "And how often have we all ignored these worn spots by merely taping the hose instead of replacing it?" I asked.

I then labeled each of these worn spots for him. I called the first worn spot "cost of goods sold," the second one "accounts receivable," the third, "inventory," and the fourth spot "sales expenses." He recognized the terms all right, but still did not see how the terms related to a worn garden hose.

"What would happen if we connected the hose to the faucet and turned the pressure up to induce more water through it?" I asked. He concluded, predictably, that some of these worn spots might leak.

But I saved until last one final spot on the hose – the end at the nozzle. We agreed that the additional water pressure would increase the output from the nozzle. I then told him, "So let's now call that nozzle "profit."

He now understood that by adding additional water pressure to the hose, the worn spots might break into larger leaks and the result would be a weaker stream from the nozzle. Moving from a hose nozzle to a business cycle, weaker profits would result from a well-intended incentive program.

The CEO got the point. He could now visualize his business cycle in the form of a garden hose.

I warned him that more sales right now might adversely affect the sales flow, much as too much water pressure can burst through worn spots on a hose. Sales flow, too, can have fatigue points, and I told him we needed to identify those points at his firm. I got his attention.

Having a garden hose in your briefcase prompts strange reactions from your seatmates on airplanes, but it also prompts good discussion – on airplanes as well as client conference rooms.

## Starting with key questions

Companies implementing an incentive program should start with a simple flow chart depicting the cycles and flows of the business. Room for improvement exists in every situation, from improved or expanded resources to better inter-department relationships. The business cycle review leads to better decisions about the initiatives needed and in what order they should be placed.

Using a blank sheet of paper, create a flow chart that contains the primary activities within your business cycle. Here is some information that will assist you in identifying your primary activities:

- *Where do you obtain the resources (raw materials, personnel, information, etc.) that you need to complete your business cycle?*

Think about what you need to provide your product or service. For example, a consulting firm might assemble information gathered from several sources into a concise report. A manufacturer assembles several pieces of raw materials into a finished product. A distributor may add value to finished products for resale. A retailer will inventory finished goods for sale to the end-user. Companies that provide financial services combine various services into specific or packaged offerings. Almost all businesses need human resources to provide their product or service.

- *How do you obtain the resources you need to complete your business cycle?*

Think about the methods that are used to deliver your resources. If you are a consulting firm, how do you get the information that is used to create reports (i.e. electronically, through interviews, etc.) for your clients? If you are a manufacturer, whom do you rely on to deliver your raw materials? If you are a distributor or retailer, who delivers products that you purchase? If you offer financial services, how do you get up-to-date information on financial service offerings? How do you recruit human resources?

- *How do you generate sales or get new customers?*

Do you sell direct to end-users? Do you sell through distributors or retailers? Do you sell through value added resellers?

- *How is installation and after sales-support provided for your product or service?*

Do you provide product installation services? Once the product is in the hands of the end-user, who is responsible for providing customer service or training to that end-user when it is needed?

## *Your business cycle flow*

```
┌──────────────┐     ┌──────────────┐     ┌──────────────┐     ┌──────────────┐
│ Develop new  │     │ Assemble &   │     │ Sell products│     │ Ship products│
│ products;    │ ──▶ │ package new  │ ──▶ │ through      │ ──▶ │ to           │
│ purchase raw │     │ and existing │     │ distributors │     │ distributors │
│ materials    │     │ products     │     │              │     │              │
└──────────────┘     └──────────────┘     └──────────────┘     └──────────────┘
                                                                        │
                                                                        ▼
┌──────────────┐     ┌──────────────┐     ┌────────────────────────┐
│ Manage       │     │ Provide      │     │ Process distributor    │
│ accounts     │ ◀── │ distributors │ ◀── │ invoices; manage       │
│ receivable   │     │ with sales & │     │ accounts payable       │
│              │     │ marketing    │     │                        │
│              │     │ support      │     │                        │
└──────────────┘     └──────────────┘     └────────────────────────┘
```

### The take-away

**Guiding principle:** Your firm is an organization. It is a whole that is larger than the sum of its departmental parts. An incentive program aimed at making changes in one department is likely to influence changes or results in other departments. Remember the garden hose analogy.

**Solution:** The solution is an incentive program that considers all company departments, examines all business dynamics, and accounts for all incremental changes in your business cycle flow.

**Example:** Every business has areas of excellence as well as areas needing improvement. These areas can be either internal or external to your business. Improvement requires a base line of data about current activity levels before you can project improvement levels. But the research is clear. A properly structured incentive program can increase performance from 25 to by 44%.9 Regrettably, few incentive programs have all the elements to get there.

### How does your incentive program measure up?

Can you identify the name and description of each activity point and customer contact point in your company's business cycle flow? Can you draw a diagram of those points? Do you know which areas need improvement before you can launch a successful incentive program that will not burden parts of your business cycle? How much time is necessary to achieve comfortable improvement?

Once you have assembled an objective and complete flowchart of your business cycle, you will be ready to build an incentive program upon it. That step is setting objectives. But be careful what you wish for.

## End Notes

[1] Slone, R. E, Mentzer, J. & Dittmann, J. P. (2007, September) Are you the weakest link in your company's supply chain? <u>Harvard Business Review.</u>

[2] Rummler, Geary, et al. Business Maps 1.0: Visualize your organization and understand its processes and relationships. Pritchell Rummler Brache Improvement Methodology. www.pritchettnet.com.

[3] Stolovich, Harold D., PhD. et al (2002, January). Incentives, motivation, and workplace performance: Research and best practices. <u>International Society of Performance Improvement</u> (ISPI, www.ispi.org) and <u>Incentive Research Foundation</u> (www.theirf.org). Study available at www.theirf.org

# Chapter 3

## Setting Objectives: Be careful what you wish for

> *"Setting and communicating the right expectations is the most important tool a manager has for imparting that elusive drive to the people he supervises."*
> — **Andrew S. Grove, former CEO of Intel Corporation.**

It's always enjoyable to talk with people who manage incentive programs. When the conversation turns to objectives, I find they typically differ only on desired dollar goal or percentage change. Regrettably, however, such objectives typically have something in common: overly short-term results.

Short-term thinking results from several factors. Top executives dictate what they want to happen. Investors and Wall Street have expectations. Those expectations are quarterly in length, a short-term view that often seriously hampers long-term corporate development. And some aggressive sales executives want to impress their companies in hopes of getting monthly or quarterly bonuses.

But the very nature of an incentive program implies you are seeking to change things. Assuming such changes are positive, wouldn't it make sense to effect changes that yield benefits beyond the incentive program's time period?

### The Gist

In past incentive programs, did you quickly jot down objectives over a sandwich with colleagues? "Let's get a bite to eat and get this done."

If so, you likely derailed the incentive program from day one. Many incentive program objectives, even those made by established companies, are imprecise, unclear, and unrelated to the overall company strategy. Within a few pages, you will see how to avoid making those mistakes with your next incentive program objectives.

Over the years I have encountered many "let's do it over lunch" objectives that obviously were not given careful thought. Setting objectives is a step in the process that is quite important. Objectives tell your incentive participants and your company management the reasons for conducting the incentive program.

A key study on the measurement of ROI on sales incentive programs revealed how a complete set of objectives can mean real profitability.[1] When all cost factors, including account receivable payments and inventory turnover, are included, and the right benchmarks are identified for comparison, the return on investment of an incentive program is easy to identify and can be quite impressive.

## A short success story ...

A nationwide food distributor, long a user of incentives to motivate sales representatives, suddenly was beset with cash flow problems. The company had great success generating new business sales by consistently stretching sales objectives for their sales territories. These constant sales increase goals certainly caused their sales team to close more sales, but at some point that reaches a critical mass. And it did.

The market became so tight that many sales people – *to maintain their eligibility in the incentive program* – brought in new accounts with questionable credit histories. When this was discovered, the incentive objectives were recast to balance sales accounting with timely collections. This added incentive objective gave the sales force a sense of ownership of client collections, leading to better relations with their clients. The result was a vast improvement in the company's cash flow.

## ... but how one program failed

A commercial bank's business development vice president implemented an incentive program to attract new business customers. The objectives were to create new deposit growth and new business accounts. The local branch officers and business development staff began working aggressively to seek new business. The incentive program exceeded the short-term objectives for both new account openings and new deposit dollars.

But the long-term result was not so good. Dissatisfaction increased within the bank's customer community. The added accounts triggered several operational problems, prompting management to re-think pricing just eight months after the incentive program ended. Business customers were soon informed of the new, higher pricing. The thought of transferring an account only reminded customers of the difficulty of transferring a banking relationship. They felt they had been duped into doing business with the bank, and they didn't appreciate the additional charges.

## Vintage thinking can turn sour

At first glance, quickly written objectives read and sound fine. I recall meeting the vice president of sales and marketing for a west coast winery. The business was family owned and managed and the VP was one of the in-laws. We discussed his proposed incentive program. As usual, the program centered on increasing sales.

The desired sales increase is typically stated in a specific percentage or dollar amount. Sales of what products are rarely defined. I was surprised to discover that this VP had thought through the issue of what. He had targeted specific wine varieties for sale increases. He even had a good handle on the distributors that would be required to increase sales through the incentive program. I made careful note of his desires for these increases as we basked in a wonderful lunch surrounded by grape vines. What a great assignment I had landed.

After lunch, I was headed home but decided to stop at the winery operations plant where grapes are crushed and the wine bottled. I met with the operations director and told him of my lunch with his counterpart in marketing. We reviewed sales numbers for the various wine varieties to be included in the planned incentive program.

He shook his head and smiled, eyes rolling like grapes in the breeze. Being a curious sort, I asked why he reacted so. His reply was classic.

"You and I know that this is a family business. I think all their dinner table conversations must be about how to sell more wine. I get these crazy forecasts every year. Truth is, even if we could sell this much wine, we do not have the capacity in our plants to manufacture it all!"

Whoops. Talk about a wow moment.

Armed with this enlightened viewpoint, I turned back and headed straight up the hill past fields of whites and reds to the chateau to find my lunch partner. I found him enjoying a glass of after-lunch wine in the tasting room. I reported what the operations director had said. The VP confirmed, yes indeed, that amount of wine production would be nearly impossible to meet.

Oh, what a revelation.

"So why did you establish this as your sales objective, without consideration of the potential impact it may have on production?" Unfortunately, I had left my garden hose in my office; it certainly would have been helpful in this case however. "Because that's what the family wants to see in sales," he replied, "I know we won't get there. But by the time the incentive program is over, they will have moved on to something else. Sales will be whatever they will be and, unless we are below last year, I'll still have a job here."

A true story. But it has a happy ending.

I managed to convince the marketing vice president that I should meet the family members. This time, I brought my garden hose! To make this a successful incentive assignment, I had to show them a better way to establish real objectives. Together, we did that as we carefully reviewed their business cycle, using the garden hose as our model. Over the years, I am pleased to say that this winery has grown quite nicely. Their distributors became more loyal to them. Today, the winery is a major player in the wine and spirits industry.

Why do initial incentive objectives usually include some sort of sales or revenue goals? It's that pervasive "top line" perspective that is habitual, even among otherwise savvy and educated managers.

It's so much easier to gauge success from the top line. But the reality is that the top line is only one measure, especially if the bottom line worsens.

I always have to get sales-oriented executives to develop more specific numbers for their objectives. Which products? How many sales of each product? How much for each sales person? I really enjoy working with companies that involve both marketing and sales managers in developing incentive programs.

## "We want to increase buzz in the marketplace!"

Silicon Valley has countless creative, energetic marketing people working at high profile companies. One time an incentive company that was trying to bring ROI thinking to one such technology firm retained me.

We started the process by reviewing the firm's business cycle, just as I have outlined for you in this book. That process went fairly well. We uncovered some short and long-term things that needed attention for any incentive programs we would plan over the years. But when we got to the incentive objectives, we hit a wall.

The stated objective for the program, already underway, was to "increase the buzz in the marketplace." Reminding you readers that my background is in finance and banking, you can appreciate my initial reaction. How simple and cute. It certainly would be nice to increase the buzz, but my ROI glands got the best of me. I probed further.

"No, I mean what is the objective of this incentive program? What do you want to see as a result?"

The answer: "Create a buzz in the marketplace."

Perhaps it's my banker mentality, but I find it difficult to quantify buzz.

Rather than go back and forth, I just asked how this program would be measured as successful. "If we have a buzz in your marketplace now that barely buzzes, will your program be judged successful at its conclusion if it sounds more like buzzzz?" I asked, my tongue poked deep into my cheek.

They didn't know how to answer that.

This project never reached the next steps. Soon after this conversation, however, senior management asked the company's marketing executive and the incentive company team a fork-in-the-road question: What are we getting for this program? What is our ROI? I was not present for this conversation, but I am fairly certain the buzzzz answer was not offered and would not have been well received had it been.

This is not the only time something like this has happened. The executives who get involved with creating objectives for incentive programs are often the creative, motivated and driven managers. They want to show off these talents by crafting language for objectives that is more clever and creative than measurable and motivating.

Objectives like create excitement, drive sales of new products, motivate our team, and – my personal favorite – drum up new sales are all well intended. But they will fall flat when it comes time to justify the budget for these programs. That judgment time will come. So read carefully and prepare your incentive objectives with specific, measurable objectives. Save the creative wording for the communications portion of your program.

> *Their answer: "Create a buzz in the marketplace."*
> *Perhaps it's my banker mentality, but I find it*
> *difficult to quantify buzz.*

### Our California manufacturer: "More sales will *hurt* our business ... how?

After completing the garden hose exercise with the CEO of the California tool manufacturer, I assembled his management staff for an exercise to establish objectives for a *potential* incentive program. I stressed the word potential because we were still in the due diligence phase of examination. It was premature to confirm any program structure.

Our first step was to examine how incentive objectives might be used to repair rough spots in their business cycle flow.

"Well, one objective must be to increase sales," said the sales vice president with confident certainty. "Without that, why are we even meeting here?"

To a degree, he was right, so I gave him some rope.

"Okay Bill, let's make sales increase an objective," I declared, "but sales of what and by how much?" Of course, Bill was not going to over-commit in front of his colleagues. He thought about it and responded with, "Well, our industry growth projections are, on average, 6-8%, so I think that should be a benchmark for our company."

I then suggested we look at what a 6% (not 8%) increase in sales would do to their business cycle flow. I used a simple flow chart, just like the one outlined in Chapter Two, to demonstrate how sales flow through this company. We started with the box labeled raw materials and went all the way through the customer service required after a sale is completed. As we progressed, I highlighted areas where their business cycle flow might not be ready for any additional pressure.

- Vendor agreements for the raw materials to assemble additional units would need to be re-structured to ensure delivery times in accordance with customer demands.
- The cross training of personnel on the manufacturing line would have to be increased and additional staff would be needed to cover peak time periods.
- Present inventory levels of older product would need to be monitored as they might become obsolete with new product introductions.
- The line of credit with the bank might need to be increased because of slower invoice payments. Also, a sales increase would require additional cash to cover working capital.
- Equipment maintenance and possible replacements would have to be escalated to ensure limited down time.
- Additional customer service staff would be required as that department is already at maximum levels.

This short but typical business cycle list grabbed the attention of the entire management team. Each of their areas would be affected because a sales increase would have burst their business cycle hose at several places. Clearly there was some work ahead before we could pump more sales through the flow with an incentive program.

That realization led us to focus first on some preliminary, short-term objectives – fixes that had to precede any incentive program. These objectives included more than 20 changes spread across all the boxes of the business cycle flow.

A sample of some of these were:

- Obtain better vendor discounts and shipping requirements
- Hire and train personnel
- Identify equipment needs; repair and replace as needed
- Collect invoices faster

This brainstorming process allowed this management team to see all of their "what if" scenarios and thus better organize and manage them. In so doing, it made them a better team. They were surprised they could finally have their say in how the business was operating without fear of sounding as if they were asking for something to benefit just their department.

Working from the preliminary list, we then ranked each potential business cycle change. The ranking method I use is fairly simple. With each business cycle objective, working from a ranking of 1 (low) to 5 (high), we ranked the potential objectives in the following areas:

- Importance – how important is this objective to the company?

- Long/Short Term Objective – can this objective be met within one year (short-term) or is it something that would take over a year to achieve (long-term)?

- Hard or soft – is this a hard, financial type objective or a soft morale booster?

The purpose of this exercise is to get all of this information out into the open. Then a management team can judge what can be realistically incorporated into the incentive program objectives now and what can be considered for future development. Remember, an incentive program is not about having a one-year shot in the arm; such a program is a building process.

After several sessions working on this list, this management team ranked the top three objectives for their business cycle. The total score achieved by each objective listed determined the rankings.

When we broke for the day I was pleased to see glad-handing and smiles as the team left the conference room to return to their busy day. I knew they were leaving with a sense they had accomplished something significant. Indeed they had. We now had three solid objectives to begin our incentive program with!

- Increase sales by not less than 6% over last year

- Improve net profit by not less than 3% over last year

- Reduce shipping costs by not less than 7% from the total cost last year

## First identify areas for improvement

Writing objectives requires a logical process, and that process starts with identifying general areas for improvement. Let's call these your improvement statements.

For example, if you wish to improve product quality for the widgets you manufacture, you might start with a simple improvement statement such as "Improve widget quality from ten defects out of every 100 units produced, to five defects out of every 100 produced, within the next six months."

Or, a sales increase and customer retention objective combined could be stated as "Increase sales by 11% over the next 12 months, and maintain a customer retention factor of not less than 95% during the same time period."

## Ranking improvements – short-term versus long-term objectives

Unless you have unlimited resources, you can't do everything all at once. So rank your areas for improvement from one to five, five being the most important.

After that ranking, determine whether each area of improvement could be accomplished as a short-term or long-term objective.

Short-term objectives can be accomplished within a year or less. Long-term objectives can be accomplished within three years.

No universal standard exists for establishing short or long-term objectives; it's all relative to your company and its industry. But the short-term objectives that succeed could provide the needed foundation for long-term objectives to work.

## Hard objectives or soft objectives

Incentive programs must recognize the difference between hard objectives and soft objectives. Hard objectives are more common because they are relatively easier to measure.

Examples of hard objectives include:

- Increase sales
- Increase profits
- Product focused sales (you may wish to motivate sales people to sell products that are in excess inventory or near obsolescence)
- Increase productivity (output)

Soft objectives are harder to measure, but they can create both financial and non-financial returns for your company. So it is a mistake to shy away from setting soft objectives solely because measurement is less quantifiable.

Examples of soft objectives that can be measured with sound survey research are:

- Increase job satisfaction
- Improve employee morale
- Improve customer loyalty
- Building team spirit

But I've seen soft objectives that were so mushy they would escape both measurement and clarity. One established company was apparently caught up in psychobabble with objectives such as "increase excitement." Another firm's incentive program acted boldly with "motivate field sales" as a goal. Soft objectives still must be clear so participants know what is expected of them.

Closely examine your identified areas of improvement that rank three or higher. Which are hard objectives and which are soft?

So far in this chapter, you have learned about three logical steps you should take in developing objectives for your incentive program:

- Develop detailed descriptions (and rankings) of areas for improvement
- Determine whether areas of improvements fit better as short-term or long-term objectives
- Determine which areas of improvement are hard objectives or soft objectives

## Ranking the objectives

The ROI incentive process spotlights the need to rank your program objectives while being sensitive to your business cycle. Your program cannot be successful unless participants focus on the objectives established, and those objectives cannot complicate your business cycle.

Likewise, it is not realistic to think that your ROI incentive program will immediately cure all of your business problems. That's why I encourage you to start by identifying and ranking areas of improvement.

You have limited resources. One such resource is time. You may have to forgo some of the areas for improvement you cited earlier.

Choose the three objectives that scored a three or higher in your rankings of importance. It is essential that you take all the previous steps cited before selecting those highest-ranking objectives.

## Aligning objectives to mission and strategy

Now we come to a more general question: Does your objective match or complement your company's present market strategy?

When I consult with clients, initially they are focused on hard objectives. Carefully defining those is a big task, as the previous chapter on business flow outlined. Then clients typically sink into dreamy generalities, such as "we want to create a buzz in the marketplace." So I start where they are with factors they can understand: numbers, dollars, and head counts. And that's why I bring up strategy in the discussion of objectives.

Creating incentive objectives that conflict with current strategy can confuse both your internal and external customers. If confusion about strategy already exists or if your mission statement is ignored or too long to remember, the design and objectives of your incentive program can be constructed to bring your company strategy back into alignment.

But I often encounter a major problem relating the incentive program to strategy and mission statement. As hard as it is to believe, I have rarely found a corporate executive who can tell me what the firm's strategy or mission statement is. I have no doubt they spent days crafting a mission, and may have done a retreat in the boondocks to devise a strategy, but what good is a mission statement or strategy no one can remember?

Consequently, missions and strategies have become my incentive radar – something is wrong. Incentives and strategy and mission must all work well together.

If you can't remember your strategy, how can you execute any tactics? Never confuse strategy with tactics, and never launch something tactical, such as an incentive program, without it being firmly grounded in the company strategy.

The appendix includes "Ten Steps to a Good Market Strategy." But here is a quick summary. Strategy is an attitude or a discipline about how you conduct your business. Unless you write it down or use it for a screen saver, it is conceptual and invisible. You can have only one strategy for a product. No such thing as "our strategies are…" Multiple strategies mean no strategy at all.

Tactics are sensual. You can read them, click to them, hear them, smell them, taste them, listen to them, or feel them. Tactics take the discipline of strategy and execute it into action. Advertising, brochures, websites, coffee cups – and incentive programs – are tactical. Most firms have many tactics.

Consider the highly successful CarMax® operation. The company's strategy is probably to reposition all used car lots as unsavory and unreliable places that you should avoid because you can't be sure what you are buying. No CarMax ad says that, of course, but that's the likely strategy. It's an attitude about how they will operate in an aging industry of selling used cars. Among the tactics at CarMax are no-haggle pricing, uniforms for staff, and staff who greet and brief customers about how CarMax differs from the overweight cigar chompers with gold chains. You walk in and quickly realize CarMax is different. The ambiance and greeting tactics demonstrate the conceptual strategy.

The following questions can help you determine the compatibility of incentive program and company strategy:

- Does each incentive program objective complement your company mission statement?
- Does each objective support what you tell customers through your company's sales message?
- Does the objective support what is communicated to your employees?

## Reasonable and realistic objectives

Incentive program objectives should motivate participants to achieve above and beyond their normal level of performance. Objectives can be aggressive, but not impossible. Program participants must perceive your objectives as realistic.

These questions can help you assess how reasonable and realistic your objectives are:

- What are the projections or standards within your industry for the objective?
- Does a three-year history provide evidence that the objective is within reach?
- Can your internal company structure support the objective if it is met or exceeded?

## A no ambiguity zone

Your objectives must be clear and concise. Ambiguity of any kind will be a waste of time, at best, and a potential disaster, at worst. Both the participants in your incentive program and those who will provide support must understand what you are seeking to achieve.

If you can answer yes to each of the following questions, you are well on your way to clearly stated objectives.

- Does the objective have a definite start and end point?
- Can the objective be easily understood by all those who are directly and indirectly involved in the ROI incentive program?
- Will a neutral observer outside your company read your objectives and understand them?

## Measurability is critical

Each objective must be measurable. Even soft objectives can be measured.

Creating measures for your ROI incentive program is key to the short and long-term success of the program. The measurement process yields important data that shows participants and management proof of your incentive program's worth. All too often incentive program measures are calculated incorrectly, or not performed at all.

Use the following questions to consider the potential measurement process for each objective.

- Is there a measurement process already in place?
- Will a new measurement process create concerns within your organization?
- Can the measure be expressed in terms that are easy to calculate?

If a measurement process is already in place for incentive programs, will that process provide reliable measures for your new program?

Are sales numbers tracked? Are market share percentages tracked? Does customer service track the number of repeat customer calls to correct the same complaint?

For a safety incentive program, are accidents and other mishaps systemically tracked? Do you track the number of units produced compared to the number of units rejected because of defects?

Selecting the objective and the measure that you will use requires that you spend some time thinking about what the actual measurement process will involve. While you can create a financial measure for almost any objective, you must first ask yourself two key questions:

- Will this measurement process create additional work (and expense) to implement? If so, will the resulting data provide enough benefit to justify the costs and effort?
- Who must approve the ROI incentive program plans prior to implementation? Who will require status reports during the program period? What type of evidence will they be seeking as proof of program success? Do program results need to be expressed in financial terms? Non-financial terms? Both?

## Reaching for the limit

Participants in an incentive program can become easily distracted. To keep them focused, limit yourself to three program objectives per incentive program. If you are unable to do so, the following factors will help you identify your final list of one to three program objectives.

1.  Review and validate the importance rating for each objective. You may wish to choose your final objectives based on their importance rating score. Consider a mix of short-term and long-term objectives. In many cases, short-term objectives may be incremental steps toward completing long-term objectives.

2.  Consider a mix of hard and soft objectives. Although results of soft objectives may be harder to measure, the achievement of these objectives can provide some great benefits.

3.  Select objectives that can be expressed in both financial and non-financial terms. When you present your objectives in this fashion, you are more likely to gain the support of a wider audience.

## The take-away

**Guiding principle:** Objectives must be clearly stated, sensitive to your business cycle flow, and aligned with mission and strategy. Objectives must have a beginning and ending date so that measurements can be taken and success determined.

**Solution:** Set your objectives within the current limits of your business cycle but with an eye towards the future. Loading your objectives with only top line results may sound good at first, but carefully review what such incremental increases will do to your overall business operation. Then consider how you can either mitigate or eliminate any potential holes in your "garden hose."

**Example:** If your incentive objective is to increase sales, consider the entire sales cycle. Your product or service starts at some point and then flows through some sort of delivery system to be prepared for the eventual sale. Once it is sold, some kind of after-sale process begins. Consider all of these aspects for any product or service that you have included in your incentive program.

## How does your incentive program measure up?

Are your incentive program objectives measurable, i.e. are they stated in quantifiable terms? Does the program have a definite termination date by which you will measure who earned an award and who did not? Are your objectives reasonable, or will only the top 10% of your staff make the goal? Conversely, are you objectives so easy that the same old group will hit the number? An ROI incentive program seeks to alter behavior for the long-term, not just a month or quarter.

Understanding your business flow is the foundation for building realistic incentive objectives that don't burst your garden hose. But it is essential to understand fully the affects and impact you program can have on departments outside your incentive program. It's all about avoiding resentment and dissention.

## End Notes

[1] Gopalakrishna, S., (2007, September) Assessing the impact of sales incentive programs: A business perspective. Incentive Research Foundation (www.theirf.org). Dr. Gopalakrishna is a professor of marketing at the University of Missouri/Columbia.

# Chapter 4:

## The Ripple Effect: Don't make waves!

*"Nothing creates more self-respect among employees than being included in the process of making decisions."*
— **Judith M. Bardwick, author, "*The Plateauing Trap*"**

If you have just been flipping through all the chapters up to now, it's time to stop. Read Chapter Four carefully. This is perhaps the most critical stage of a successful ROI incentive program.

Companies use incentive programs to prompt change. But organizational changes ripple throughout the company, much like stones tossed across a pond.

Whether your ROI Incentive Program is focused on sales, customer service, or safety, other areas within your company may be directly or indirectly affected by the incentives. Many incentive programs identify a desired change and target the right audience. But few incentive program managers take one additional, critical step: determining if the change could disrupt other company functions outside of the program's target. Such negative effects must be identified and addressed prior to launching the incentive program.

War stories make the point. A sales manager for a home improvement products manufacturer recalls the failure of a sales incentive program that focused on new types of customers versus sales from all customers. An incentive consultant, obviously someone unfamiliar with the concept of incentive ROI, set up the program and management approved it. The top five sales representatives would earn a trip to Amsterdam.

The sales staff quickly refocused on the targeted new prospects – engineers and architects who might be persuaded to specify the company's products for construction projects.

But one of the five sales representatives who earned the trip dropped a bomb during the announcement meeting. He was heading for Holland, but his sales were heading south by 35%.

The problem with such an incentive program is that it sounds like a good idea: "Let's increase our calls on people whom we otherwise miss or people we don't often close." Sales people, by nature, are motivated by incentives. But targeting an architect in New York might mean sales in someone else's territory. An incentive program that targets new customer profiles might conflict with incentives to increase sales from current customers.

## The Gist

**Sales people and others targeted by incentive programs generally like participating in them. But their colleagues in other departments often resent how their workday is affected by incentives. Preventing such resentment is important. The first step is recognizing the ripple effects your incentive program has on other parts of your company. Such knowledge and awareness can create new areas of profit and cash flow and prevent those same profits and dollars from leaking away.**

So much information is available to help you avoid incentive program blunders. The Incentive Research Foundation regularly surveys the world of incentives and commissions research on what is working and what is not. One of their studies ranks the effectiveness of various types of incentive programs: [1]

- Quota based incentive programs were reported as most effective. This is an incentive given for reaching or exceeding a performance goal.
- Piece rate incentive programs were considered next in effectiveness, but such incentives are seen as significantly less effective than quota incentives. A piece rate program awards more for increasing the rate of performance or doing more of something, such as increasing the production rate per hour or day of a specific item.
- Tournament incentives were far less effective than piece rate incentives. In a tournament, individuals or teams compete with each other.

The same study outlines five conditions needed for an effective incentive program:

1. Current performance on specific work goals is inadequate.

2. The cause of the inadequate performance is motivational (rather than due only to a lack of knowledge and skill or to environmental barriers).

3. The desired performance type and level can be quantified (how much, how often, how many).

4. The goal is challenging yet achievable (easy goals are not appropriate).

5. The organization requires that all other performance goals continue to be achieved at or above current levels.

### A short success story…

Managers at an insurance company with a history of successful incentive sales programs surveyed employees and were startled with the results. Non-sales employees resented incentive programs because added sales increased their workload. Only sales reps were rewarded for increases, not the support staff.

Management was stuck. They could not eliminate incentives for sales reps but knew that incentives for non-sales employees would never be approved.

The incentive team wisely decided to include other departments in the planning of all future incentive programs. They began by asking each department a simple question: If we implement an incentive program designed to achieve the following objectives, what affect would that have on your department?

The new planning sessions helped spotlight the additional resources each department needed. They also identified new revenue sources not previously uncovered. Thereafter, non-sales department employees backed the program because their opinions and positions were suddenly influential.

## ... but how one program failed

A pharmaceutical company sponsored annual sales incentive programs to increase market share and introduce new products. The programs included incentive awards for both the outside sales force and the inside telesales team. Management wanted both sales forces motivated.

Sales projections were made, but the incentive program benchmarks were higher than projected sales for three new products. As expected, sales of those three products exceeded the projections. That made executives very happy.

Unfortunately, other departments reported poor operating performance. The incentive program's sales increases overloaded their staffs, prompting calls for additional hires. Overtime wage costs increased in almost every department. Overnight shipping costs shot up as sales representatives tried to qualify for last minute incentive points. Morale decreased among employees working 24/7 schedules. In short, the costs of the problems outweighed the increased revenue.

I am always amazed at the reaction I get when I approach departments not directly involved in a company's incentive program and seek their suggestions. If you read this chapter and have these discussions, you will be amazed at the reactions you receive.

You are probably thinking, "I don't want to open up Pandora's box by approaching these departments. I may not like what I hear and it might sink my incentive program." Here is the reality: If you don't ask, your incentive program will surely sink. It is not a question of if your incentive program will eventually falter, but rather when that will happen.

Let's get back to our manufacturing case study to see how I persuaded the company's management team to become involved and fully engaged in the incentive program.

## Our California manufacturer: "But what happens if...?"

At this point in the ROI incentive planning for our California manufacturer, the CEO began to understand why we could not leap into an incentive program without further data. But the process had to include more than just a review of their business cycle and stated objectives. We also needed to examine the financial results of our proposed incentive program.

As you read earlier in this case study, a sales increase was one of the incentive program's objectives. Using that as my starting point, I set out to follow up on the short-term objectives the management team identified and ranked during the business cycle review. As you have already learned, this session uncovered several areas within the company that would be affected by the incentive program. Using the sales objective we had all agreed to, I began this part of my ROI process by asking the big question: If – and I stressed the word if – we implemented a sales incentive program to increase sales by 6%, how might that affect your department?

That sounds like an easy question to ask and answer, but this is one step in my process that I never want to eliminate. I asked the same question of the department heads in finance, operations, human resources, marketing, and purchasing. Several activities in each department needed to be considered before further incentive plans could be implemented.

But a shocker was uncovered. These department managers were surprised even to be asked about incentive program consequences in their areas. I think several of them thought their participation was concluded after we ended the business cycle discussion on objectives. But now they would have even more input to provide.

Not only did each department manager see this as an olive branch from the sales department, each also viewed this as an opportunity to address their areas of concern. Previously, such areas of concern were never discussed at meetings because the managers saw incentive programs as solely the turf of the sales department. They assumed their added expenses didn't seem important to sales.

But those issues were finally raised, and they were now important to the success of the incentive program.

The finance and accounting staff had been struggling with their customer billing process. The manager had investigated new software but he couldn't justify the expense. When we discussed an incremental sales increase, however, we were able to project new revenue that could be used to fund such software.

Remember, our objective was to increase sales, but with that was the need to invoice new sales and then collect payment. They go together. In the end, the software proved to be a good short and long-term investment. We added the software's cost into our projected ROI incentive budget plan.

The human resources manager was concerned about the added volume that comes with added sales. How many trained employees would be needed and how would we find them? We worked with the HR to identify how many people were needed and what training was needed. We then added those expenses into our ROI incentive plan budget.

The operations manager was concerned about production equipment. While routine maintenance had been performed, some equipment was past the glue and bandage stage. Major repairs or replacements would be needed. When we projected the added stress of the incremental sales on that equipment, it was easy to see what had to be done to prepare for our incentive increase in sales. Again, we added these additional expenses into our ROI incentive plan.

My meeting with the purchasing manager proved insightful. This manager revealed that for years he had been struggling with providing accurate cost accounting information for the executive team. This was not part of the job when he was hired. As the company grew, he had to learn more and more about the cost function. He was struggling just to keep his head above water. I asked if he ever considered hiring a cost accountant to relieve him. His answer was predictable: no budget. We added this significant staff addition into our ROI incentive plan budget. But when I left his office, I knew he had doubts he would ever see this new hire.

Of no surprise was the welcome reception from the marketing manager. She thought that having these discussions was a grand idea long overdue. It was nice to have that start to our discussion. She wanted to introduce some new elements, but they fell under the budget radar. So we worked through how those new items could be incorporated into the incentive program. Once again, those expenses were added to our ROI incentive plan budget.

In addition to these key departments, I also met with the company sales manager. Believe it or not, he too was surprised that I included him in this process! He thought I would just be talking to the other departments about his sales incentive. That was true, but I also needed to know what incremental sales expenses would be generated from the effort to increase sales, such as increased travel and entertainment (T&E), commissions, and office expenses. These costs were added to our ROI incentive plan budget.

At the conclusion of this step in my incentive ROI process, this manufacturing company now had a far more complete vision of the financial consequences that would result from a 6% increase in sales. They could now determine whether an incentive program was a good or bad investment. The figures showed this company would yield more than enough financial return to proceed to the next steps in my incentive ROI process.

**How this came about and why you cannot ignore having these discussions!**

At this point you are rolling your eyes and saying, "No way we're going through all this."

Hold off…give me a chance to convince you. I am most passionate about this part of the ROI process. It is the very place where this entire ROI concept and method came to me in the first place.

I had enjoyed several good years in the incentive business. I operated some very high-end incentive travel programs for some of the largest companies in the world. I became involved in the incentive travel industry because I saw the true business application of it all – increase sales (and profit) by motivating the sales team with a great incentive award and then fund that incentive budget using a percentage of the increase in sales. It made sense to me.

But I am sad to say that, even today, most incentive programs tend to adopt more of a "save me money" focus rather than a "make me money" focus. In 1990, I found that out the hard way. With this book, I intend to save you from falling into that same trap. Let me share another war story with you.

After completing a rather exotic incentive travel experience for one of my clients, I was asked to visit with the vice president of sales and marketing to discuss next year's program. A good sign, I thought, especially because the economy wasn't robust at that time.

But the meeting hit a thud. The discussion was all about how I could provide the client with another great travel experience – like we just had. Then I got *The But Word*. It's a word that is deadly in these conversations. They wanted the same experience … but with a budget that would be 30% less.

Huh? Impossible, I thought.

I used every stretch of my own sales skin to gain an audience with the CEO. It wasn't easy, but luckily I had a relationship there. I confirmed with him that he anticipated a program with the same number of participants, the same hotel quality activities, and the same number of days – but at 30% fewer budget dollars, right?

Oh, I wish I could tell you that this highly acclaimed CEO saw what I saw and finally agreed we could not provide a Mercedes Benz experience on a Volkswagen budget. No, he did not.

His stance forced me to ask a very direct question: "How can I do that for you"? He gave me an equally direct yet flattering answer for which I am still thankful. In fact, his answer launched me into a whole new direction *that led directly to this book*.

### "Bob, you're a smart guy. You will figure this out."

And so I have. I started by referring this valuable but now unprofitable client to a new incentive awards source. Then I proceeded to perform my own investigation with the blessing of the CEO. I went back over the three years of what the client and I thought were program successes. I wanted to see what happened below the revenue line.

It was a revelation. I assembled the desired top line numbers, but then had to add chaos and losses below. Bad attitudes about the incentive programs permeated those departments that struggled to maintain their own positions in the company as I forced more sales through the business cycle. Remember the leaky garden hose?

I had these same discussions with three other companies where I had previously focused on providing sales increases. The results were all the same. The problems I helped to create – *by just focusing on the sales line* – came back to hurt these firms about 18 months later. It was a wake-up call.

These inter-department discussions with key managers must be incorporated into your incentive planning process unless you have a plan to keep juggling your incentive budget every year, as some firms do. The other option is to hope that your incentive provider will magically find a way for you get a great deal on the same program benefits for substantially less.

Do you really believe you can make that happen in your company?

### What to ask your internal management team

These internal discussions will uncover information that will affect your incentive program's rules structure. The outcome of these discussions, and how you adjust your proposed incentive program, can generate support from these same key departments. This can occur even though these departments may not directly participate in the award portion of your incentive program.

Some good questions to consider include:

- What are the key departments within your company?
- Who is the key decision-maker or manager within each of these departments?
- Could your incentive program adversely affect these departments' normal operations?
- What additional resources would your department need before absorbing the affects of this incentive program?
- When could you department absorb the incentive program's goals and what is needed?

Ready to start knocking on those other department doors? Do you wonder how the discussion might go?

> *He had almost no hope of collecting more than*
> *$2 million in invoices.*
> *Then I felt the big one hit. "And for that you sent our*
> *sales team to Thailand for a week."*

## Finance and accounting

Incentive programs significantly affect finance and accounting. For one thing, your incentive program has a budget with short-term costs. But how you design your incentive program can determine whether you end with a return on your incentive investment.

In a sales incentive program, revenue is supposed to increase. But cost of goods sold can change, and thus gross profits. Operations and fulfillment expenses rise to absorb the sales increase. Will new account activity create work for your credit department and accounts receivable staff? Will new orders from existing customers affect their discounts? These are not the kind of surprises you want your CFO to discover. Having these discussions will help you to uncover all true costs that identify real ROI, a concept your CFO will appreciate.

When I did my very first attempt at this, it was with a finance manager. He really startled me about how incentives can affect accounting and finance departments. He reported how the incentive program that I had managed for them had definitely increased sales for the company.

I thought I was safe. Oh, was I wrong.

"Sixteen months after the program ended," he said tersely, "I am still trying to collect invoices from some of these new customers." He leaned forward in his chair with arms folded guardedly across his chest and summed it up for me. He had almost no hope of collecting more than $2 million in invoices. Then I felt the big one hit. "And for that you sent our sales team to Thailand for a week."

That moment would have been a perfect time to film an airline commercial, like the commercials that say, "Want to get away?" I surely did. But it was a learning experience.

## Human resources

Will additional staff, either permanent or temporary, be needed to accommodate your incentive program objectives? Are other incentive programs already operating – bonus plans, employee recognition programs – that your program could clash with and thus confuse participants in both programs?

This is especially common if one incentive program seeks new customers while another program seeks add-on sales from existing customers. Which one should gain the attention of the sales force?

It is not uncommon to have several incentive programs happening at the same time. Some departments call them other things, but if they are intended to change behaviors, they are incentive programs.

One such situation demonstrates how this conflict can really adversely affect your program. The company had instituted an incentive program they called an employee initiative. The objective was to reduce overtime. They wanted the incentive presented in a positive light rather than the traditional call for "no more OT." That was a great intention and the program had a good start.

But then the incentive sales program began to create the need for overtime. The conflict between the sales and operations managers, with the human resources manager acting as referee, was pale in comparison to how confused the employees were regarding which incentive to pursue.

A more significant issue is whether your proposed incentive program conflicts with the existing compensation plan. As is stressed often in this book, an incentive program confused with compensation is an ineffective incentive program.

## Operations

Most companies have limited resources. Does your company have the capital resources to handle any additional volume created by your incentive program? Do you have operational capacity and trained personnel to handle added volume? Are raw materials available at an acceptable cost to support higher volume, and can you receive them at regular shipping rates? Can your quality control staff manage additional volume without compromising your reputation? Is post-sale customer support, such as customer training, capable of scheduling the extra work?

If your ROI incentive program is likely to generate additional expenses, such as for new plant equipment, you must involve your operations and finance departments to determine the short and long-term financial implications. Accounting for such expenses must be done during the incentive program's operating period.

While most incentive program plans consider the overall operational capacity, capacity is not the only issue. You need to remember, in the end, it is the people who get the job done.

I have seen how a well-designed incentive program can lead to a hectic environment where safety and wellness of the employees are at stake. Make sure, during your discussions with the operations manager, that the production team is fully staffed and armed with all of the tools they need (including training) to be able to handle any additional volume generated by your incentive program.

## Sales and marketing

Conflicting incentive programs are commonplace, especially in companies with multiple selling channels. You must determine if other sales related incentive programs, either within your company or at one of your suppliers or customers, would conflict with your proposed program.

The big picture of marketing messages is equally important. Could your incentive program message clash with your firm's overall sales or marketing message? If so, your program confuses the sales ranks.

Most of us think sales and marketing staffs are in tune with each other. But that tune can quickly go flat, especially if the company sells into multiple markets.

A great example of this is the automotive industry. The manufacturer offers incentives to both dealership owners and to consumers. Usually, there are several layers of incentive. The ownerships know what they have to do to earn their manufacturer's incentive. A dealer's general manager knows what he or she has to do to gain the manufacturer's incentive. Then the dealership sales manager will undoubtedly implement "spiffs" each week or month in order to achieve the sales goals. Lastly, we consumers march in to ask about our incentives. Think there can be any confusion here?

## Customer service and returns

An increase in new sales activity should lead to production increases. But even if no change occurs in product quality, increases in shipments will also likely generate an increase in returns or customer service activity. Can your returns department and customer service staff handle additional call or service volumes? If not, how long will it take for them to become ready for extra volume?

Most of us recognize there is fierce competition today for tele-communications, cell phone service, internet service and, of course, cable versus satellite TV. The sales teams for these companies are very involved in incentives. This industry resembles the automotive industry in their approach to incentives. Ever try to get new cable service just before football season? No problem finding someone to sign you up for it, but then try and get a technician to come out an install it before kickoff! This front end loading of sales creates a lot of top line revenue, but a great deal more ill will on the back end. Would you really want to be that installation technician?

## Incentive good will

These interviews will yield valuable information on departments' strengths and weaknesses. You may be the only person in the company, other than top executives, to be so familiar with the firm's operational managers and their domains. You asked their opinions. You listened. And they likely were flattered. Those interviews may form the good will capital that could ease the acceptance of many more incentive programs.

### The take-away

**Guiding principle:** Having inter-department discussions about your incentive program is an essential part of due diligence. Gaining the insight and support of all departments within the organization is a pre-requisite to launching ROI incentive programs.

**Solution:** Asking for inter-departmental insights and support can actually enhance the relations among departments and strengthen the incentive mentality. Open and frank discussions about "what if" scenarios will spotlight hidden costs and revenues that might be addressed by the incentive program. Such a discussion builds a positive environment for non-incentive departments in the company and can eliminate the need to provide incentive awards for everybody. When non-targeted departments are consulted before the incentive program is launched, they feel connected and involved and will better understand what's expected of them.

**Example:** Many incentive managers view all this as unnecessary. Some managers suffer from silo thinking, asking "Why would we want to ask other departments about *our* incentive program? After all, those other departments have a job to do and they had better do it," they might assert. But the stories in this chapter should provide you with solid answers to these objections. The cost of flying happy sales people to Thailand added to the cost of $2 million in receivables is hard to justify.

## How does your program measure up?

Have you even interviewed other departments about a pending incentive program? If not, you are missing a valuable opportunity. This is an ideal way to gain acceptance for your incentive program. Don't fear this process; embrace it. Don't think that these other areas of the company will want to get in on your incentive awards budget. Just having their concerns heard will more than reward them.

Knowing how you program affects other departments is important. But what about factors outside your company? You don't operate in a vacuum.

## End Notes

[1] Stolovich, H., Clark, R. & Condly, S. (2002, January). Incentives, motivation and workplace performance; Research and best practices. The International Society for Performance Improvement and the Incentive Research Foundation (IRF). www.theirf.org.

# Chapter 5:

## External environment: What they do affects you, too

> *"One of the soundest rules I try to remember when making forecasts in the field of economics is that whatever is to happen is happening already."*
>
> — **Sylvia Porter**

Your company does not operate in a vacuum. Several external factors, outside your control, can affect your company. But you already know that.

What you don't know is that wonderfully designed incentive plans can be destroyed by outside influences. Even though you cannot control them, you can plan for them and build your ROI incentive program around their potential effects. Chapter Five will help you anticipate such unknowns.

External factors include your competitors, government regulations, and the economy. I continue to be amazed at how often these factors are ignored – *especially in building an incentive program.*

Some questions you should consider before launching an ROI incentive program:

- Who are your competitors and what are they doing to increase sales in your regions?
- Who are your customers' alternative sources, i.e. suppliers that are not direct competitors?
- What economic factors affect your business?
- What economic factors affect your customers' businesses?
- What economic indicators help you plan for your business?
- What government regulations affect your business?
- What proposed legislation could affect your business?
- What is your professional trade association predicting?

## The Gist

**Launching an incentive program without an up-to-date review of potential outside forces and influences is like believing your organization operates in a vacuum. The competitive environment, economic developments, and pending government actions can affect your program's success – adversely or positively. Such a review is especially important if your business sells in multiple regions that could be affected differently by such external factors.**

## A short success story...

A nationwide automotive repair and maintenance company conducted annual incentive programs that rewarded employees on several factors, from improving customer service ratings to gathering intelligence about competitors. Employees were encouraged to submit information about competitors, from marketing ads to news stories. The firm's marketing team used such information to supplement wider industry news.

As the company's incentive program unfolded, new legal mandates emerged that would greatly affect automotive repair and maintenance businesses. Management began to educate their local managers on how to deal with the changes. Employees gathered information that revealed competitors in several key markets seemed unaware of the mandates. By forecasting the legal changes, management could design an incentive program that took advantage of competitors' lack of foresight. Consequently, the company gained market share in a year when many competitors lost share or closed their doors.

## ... but how one program failed

A nationwide real estate company implemented an incentive program to attract new listings and customer referrals. The program included all franchise regions, but the program's design failed to consider the differing economic climates among the regions. Regions experiencing a real estate boom soared past program objectives, while depressed regions failed even to meet minimum objectives.

A survey of the firm's agents and a review of the incentive planning process revealed mistakes. Regional objectives were obviously not aligned with local economic realities. Several agents commented on the changing climate in their region and how the company seemed unaware of competitive forces. Consequently, agents in depressed regions never participated in the incentive program because they saw no way to achieve the objectives.

## Oh, but this chapter doesn't apply to me?

Right now, you are probably reacting to all this much the way many of my clients have reacted to the topic of external influences. "You're joking...you're telling me I have to review economic indicators and government legislation just to have my sales team win a trip to Hawaii?"

Yes, that's exactly what you need to do ....*if you want the incentive program to earn a return on your investment in it.*

If the thought of return on investment prompts visions of financial statements, have no fear. Rather, we are about to review how to use economic indicators to predict - that's right, predict - your incentive program's success.

Let me explain how I approached this with our California case study company. After you see how the CEO and his team lived through this analysis, you will not be so hesitant to read further.

## Our California manufacturer: "*We're not doing this in a vacuum....*"

After my visits with each department manager to discuss their "what if" scenarios for the sales increase objectives, I came back to the CEO and briefed him on the next steps in my ROI process. We would now look at the various external factors that may influence or affect our incentive program.

- Economic indicators: How will the national, local, or regional economy play a part in our sales forecast and, more importantly, what if anything can we do about it?
- Competitive environment: How will your competitors react to your incentive program?

The CEO thought they had been managing external factors well. But after a brief conversation with his key managers in the conference room, I thought otherwise. Listen in:

"I monitor what is happening by reading the trades and listening to my sales team," said the vice president of sales, "and I read the *Wall Street Journal.*" I leaned across the conference table and smiled, saying, "But by the time that news is 'news,' it is usually too late to do much about it."

I could almost hear him gulp.

"I don't track economic indicators, per se," said the CFO. "I mostly compare our monthly and yearly financial trends against budget." So I asked her what happens to her sales forecast if a direct industry indicator, such as housing starts, drops 40% in a three month period?"

She got the point. So did the managers in human resources, marketing, and purchasing.

They had some information about their top three competitors, but something was shallow about that data. I needed more nuance. Each deeper question I asked prompted more head scratching than discussion. These were not hard questions, nor was I attempting to uncover deep dark secrets about their competitors. But except for the sales manager, the others were not jumping to reply.

What I found with this company is what I have encounter with most companies at this stage in the ROI incentive process. They have some surface knowledge of their competitive environment, but not much more.

> *"I monitor what is happening by reading the trades and listening to my sales team," said the vice president of sales, "and I read the Wall Street Journal."*
>
> *I leaned across the conference table and smiled, saying, "But by the time that news is 'news', it is usually too late to do much about it."*

Only the sales manager was responding to my questions. After many minutes of this, I noticed the other managers were glancing back and forth. Then one of them asked if they were really needed in this meeting as the others gingerly rose from their chairs.

"Yes," I responded quickly with a theatrical show of surprise. They soon realized why they were indeed an important part of the sales incentive process. As a group, we began to examine the company's history of competing in the marketplace.

We all agreed everyone was chasing the same customer. We focused on how to gain management's insights into the strengths and weaknesses of each competitor and, more importantly, how the team could exploit those factors.

We examined our win-loss record. How often do we win when we go head to head with these guys? When we lose, why do we lose? Do we act on anything that we learned from losing the business?

After a few minutes, the team was acting as if they had gathered all the competitive information that was needed. That's when I moved to a different aspect of their competitive environment. Two simple questions led to dead silence.

First, I asked if they saw any changes on the economic horizon. Then I asked if any government legislation was pending. The scratching heads reappeared. Answers to these two questions were a mystery to this management team.

It never ceases to amaze me. Here we were making plans to grow sales of this company. But before I raised such questions in their conference room, these highly qualified managers were ready to launch incentives without knowing how market forces – *beyond their control* – might make or break their program. I wasn't trying to complicate this discussion; I kept it simple.

Reality Check: Think about this conference room scene. Is this how you plan and operate incentives?

I now had their attention. First, we reviewed their customers' economic climate. This manufacturer sells its hand tools to companies that are involved in new home and remodel construction across the United States. Regions differ. I was not surprised that we gathered responses that differed among the regions. In areas where homes were being built at a rapid pace and existing homes were being remodeled, the company enjoyed higher demand for its products. In less robust construction climates, we noted lower margins from competitive pressure on discount.

Next I introduced the management team to a simple economic forecasting tool that begins with crystal ball questions: What if you could see your company's future 3-4 months ahead? Would you change anything about your business?

Silly? Actually, the management team soon realized such forecasting would benefit not just incentive planning but all company planning.

The forecasting started with a discussion about sales because that topic grabs management's attention. We listed monthly sales for the past five years.

Next, we discussed the economic indicators that the team agreed could affect their business. An obvious indicator for them is housing starts. Now we had two columns of related figures: sales history and housing starts for the past five years.

Can you see where this is going yet? We had assembled data that could help us predict an increase or a decrease in sales. Our brief analysis indicated that when housing starts begin to decline, tool sales declined within three months.

We used this and other indicators to measure our incentive program against the economy. This review made it possible to answer the question most incentive managers can't answer: "How do we know it was the incentive program and not the economy that caused the change to happen?" It also would help us develop a level playing field in the incentive rules structure to accommodate changes among the regions' economies.

No real government issues were uncovered in the meeting. But that topic prompted good comments about how new regulations could change market conditions and how the company might respond. The decisions of the Federal Reserve Board are a good example here.

The group concluded that real forces and factors existed that could dictate what they could sell and at what prices they could sell. Lastly, we summarized our findings and targeted additional data to be tracked that could help us attribute any incremental change to the incentive program.

The scratching heads that earlier wanted to leave the meeting departed with broad smiles. We all felt like field generals who had plotted their tanks and troops against enemy forces as they slept unawares.

References and examples of this process are in the appendix. I recommend you review them and go to my website (wwww.businessgroupinc.com) for more information and an interactive exercise called the incentive ROI Optimizer™.

## Your competitive environment

Let's move on to your company because, by now, you wondering if your incentive program might fail.

And well it could.

How much is known about your company competitors and how they have reacted to external influences? You must assume they are analyzing your history and studying your distribution model, so your internal incentive team should do likewise.

Identify the top three to five competitors in your marketplace. Make sure you leave a place for the often illusive and invisible competitor X. That's the alternative source from which your customers can buy that may not be a direct competitor. This is increasingly common in an Internet savvy world.

Some important questions to ask:

- What do your competitors do really well? Where do they out-perform you? How does your company address this?

- What are your competitors' weaknesses? How does your company exploit these weaknesses?

- Do these companies compete with you in all product lines and regions? If not, where do they and why? How successful is your company when competing head to head on the same business?

- Have any changes occurred in your competitive environment in the past three years that have affected your company either positively or negatively?

- Are any changes anticipated in your company's competitive environment?

- Are you keeping track of Internet marketing developments, such as blogs, that could affect your e-commerce and other sales channels?

Several simple methods can be used to obtain accurate information regarding your competitors:

- Interview sales professionals in your company.

- Survey your customers.

- Survey your prospective customers.

- Purchase goods and services from your competitors.

- Research industry publications for articles and news stories about your competitors.

- Review your monthly trade journals, especially issues that survey member companies.

- Ask editors of trade journals what's happening and how they see the future.

- Never miss the major trade show in your industry. Watch customer traffic in competitors' exhibits. Attend key sessions. Listen carefully to all conversations. Ask provocative questions.

## Your economic environment

All companies operate within an environment that is subject to some economic movements, either up or down. It is important to recognize the economic indicators for your business and to consider them when developing your ROI incentive program objectives.

Some important questions to ask:

- What is the current economic climate of your customers?

- What economic factors are important in your business? What are the key indicators for those factors? How regularly do you access information about those indicators?

- How does the economic climate differ from one region to another?

- How has your company responded to good and bad economic indicators? Has your response to movements been consistently effective? Do you have a contingency plan for responding?

## Government legislation

Few industries are immune from government actions and influence. Your company is not likely one of them.

Government legislation and regulations pertaining to your business and industry can significantly influence how you operate your business -- and your ultimate success.

Government agencies and watchdogs are especially vigilant about anything to do with food, health, or the environment. And they don't necessarily care whether you succeed in business or not.

In addition to considering legislation that affects you directly, make sure you also consider legislation that can affect your customers, suppliers, and other business partners. Such legislation will likely affect your business.

Be sure to ask these questions:

- Is there any legislation pending at the national, state, or local level that will affect my business or industry?

- Is an international trade agreement, such as NAFTA, likely to be signed or amended that could affect your business?

- Are developments in key economies, such as the Middle East, India, China, or Russia, likely to impact your business?

If you don't know the answers, contact someone at your industry's trade association. If you have not joined such an association, it may be time. The world is changing. Nearly all large trade associations have lobbyists who are paid to keep track of legislators and powerful zealots.

## The take-away

**Guiding principle:** All influential economic, political, and social factors and trends must be considered in setting incentive program objectives. Competitive forces, price changes, government legislation, and the economy can all affect results. Including these external indicators in your ongoing incentive program measures of success will greatly enhance your program success.

**Solution:** Contingency planning is essential. An incentive program must reflect the real world in which your employees operate. They do not operate in a world totally under your control. They operate in a highly competitive world, governed by agencies that care little about your business as we all float in a world economy that is constantly changing. An incentive program can be a feather in the hurricane in such a world.

**Example:** How will you answer the question that I know you will get: "How do we know it was the incentive program that caused this positive result to happen?"

## How does your program measure up?

If you have no contingency plan that routinely assesses competitive forces, such a plan is a good place to start constructing an incentive program. The same is true of contingencies for handling economic changes or new governmental actions. The questions posed earlier in this chapter will help you make your program measure up to ROI success.

Inter-department discussions to be sure you are not causing a ripple inside your company. External forces that can affect your program. Sounds complete, right? But what about perceptions ... your employees' perceptions of an incentive program? Guess those wrong and your program falters from the start. Let's tackle those perceptions in Chapter Six.

# Chapter 6:

# Lining Up Perceptions: What you think ... versus what they think.

Tom Peters has it right. We humans have an immediate perception of anything that is marketed to us. Some companies are blessed with positive public perceptions of their products. Others struggle to overcome negative reputations even after their products have measurably improved.

Perceptions can kill an incentive program. Never launch one without first assessing the attitudes and perceptions of participants. They have perceptions about their compensation, their experience with past incentive programs, their reactions to awards ... and their perception of management and the company. And all those perceptions are sticky.

Researchers have studied perceptions and expectations. A body of knowledge called expectancy theories suggests that an employee's effort exerted in pursuit of a award is positively related to the perceived value of the award. Social psychologists have done research that suggests participants may perceive non-monetary incentives as more valuable than the cash value of the award.

Employee perceptions drive the willingness to participate – their engagement level – in an incentive program. Research indicates groupings based on gender or tenure or functions have no relationship to a group's willingness or engagement.[1]

But company strategies and policies have much more influence on employee engagement. According to the same study, the degree of emotional engagement is four times more influential on employee motivation than an employee's rational engagement. Emotions drive perceptions, rightly or wrongly.

Motivation affects employee turnover, not just participation in incentive programs. One research study showed that higher levels of motivation can translate into a 53% reduction in employee attrition. [2]

Employee satisfaction drives employee engagement, according to a study of 100 organizations.[3] The study concluded that when individuals and teams compete to accomplish marketplace goals and to please customers, such competition works to the benefit of both their employers and their customers.

These pages have revealed many stories of incentive programs that appeared successful until problems arose that were quite costly. Assuming the production staff can handle extra orders is one such problem. Assuming anything about your targeted incentive program participants is equally inadvisable. You may be close to announcing your incentive program rules and choosing participant awards, but the rules and the awards must rest on sound information.

> ## The Gist
>
> **Launching an incentive program without first assessing targeted participants' attitudes about incentives is a big mistake. Never assume anything about possible participants. In this chapter you will learn what data to gather and how to use it to ensure incentive program success.**

Although it's long been a common sense observation, now research indicates that employees' perception and engagement can influence a business's success.[4] If management satisfies basic employee needs, such as compensation and workplace environment, employees become more motivated to do a good job. The result is reduced employee turnover and reduced recruiting and training costs.

In Chapter One we saw how our California tool manufacturer was advised to build a solid foundation for his incentive program by first making sure the company had a solid compensation plan in place. Having a good compensation foundation means that your employees, both those who may be directly involved in your incentive award plans and those who will be asked to provide support of your incentive program, believe they are fairly compensated for doing their expected level of performance. The purpose of any incentive program, however, is to exceed normal expectations and to reward those who do that.

Satisfied employees communicate better with customers and thus reduce customer turnover, too. Research indicates that effective managers recognize that employees may know better how to improve the customers' positive experience with the business.[5] That begins by asking employees, "What is the biggest problem you face day in and day out as you try to deliver high quality service to our customers?"

So at this stage in ROI incentive planning, we start gathering baseline data about the likely participants.

Success is a function of measurement; measurement is a function of having all the right information. Without baseline data at the start of the program, how can you evaluate real program success at its termination?

This baseline is the line of sight for everyone, both incentive program managers and incentive participants. For managers, the baseline is often surprising. It compares management's perceptions of the incentive program to participants' perceptions. Long ago, I stopped being surprised by the disparity between them.

For example, before you can ask participants to exceed normal expectations through an incentive program, you must determine if they have the knowledge, support, training, and tools to do their jobs today – without the incentive program. If employees lack those elements, how can an incentive program be worth the investment?

Oftentimes, management believes the targeted employees are competitively compensated. But if employees do not perceive their compensation as competitive, they will likely react to an incentive program with a response such as "They should just give us extra money in our checks." Any mismatches can negatively affect your incentive program.

It is also essential to gauge accurately where the incentive participants are on their personal hierarchy of needs. Psychologists have long studied how people progress – in sequence – from basic needs, such as paying their bills, to higher level needs, such as recognition and personal satisfaction. If incentive participants believe they have been mistreated or short-changed, research indicates that no award will inspire them until trust is restored or they regain job satisfaction.

Also, many companies launch programs without first determining if public recognition will work better than cash. Cash is spent. Recognition has staying power. Really successful sales people with high incomes may be well beyond cash as motivation if they now stand on the top step of their hierarchy of needs.[6]

### A short success story...

The call center for a vacation time-share company routinely launched several types of incentive programs throughout the year. These programs were introduced during both high and low selling seasons. Incentive objectives were measured by such criteria as duration of call, number of calls made, closing ratio, and customer satisfaction rating.

After operating these incentive programs for six months, management noticed an alarming disparity. One calling group performed consistently above target, while another group was ranged from below target to at target levels. Interviews with the successful team members indicated they had the right product information and other tools to process more calls, close more transactions, and earn customer praise. Management wanted to know how the entire calling group liked the available sales tools, their work environment, and their training. Most important, did they understand the importance of the objectives upon which they were measured.

Management was hit with a big surprise! Survey results indicated successful team members did not think they had sufficient product and marketing knowledge. So, prior to the next program implementation, management ran educational workshops and produced marketing tools team members could use daily. As part of the incentive program, team members earned additional award points for mentoring others or sharpening their own sales skills. Management conducted surveys throughout the incentive program to assess team satisfaction, enabling both management and participants to be on a level playing field regarding expectations.

### ... but how one program failed

A retail catalog company created an incentive program for customer service center employees. The program was implemented in response to several months of weak customer service ratings. After analyzing the customer service ratings and reviewing potential incentive awards, key supervisors decided on a selection of awards they believed would motivate their customer service team to perform better.

But after several months, customer service levels had not improved. Team morale was poor.

Several employees eventually left the company after the ratings continued downward. In exit interviews, departing employees talked about the incentive program. They even said they wished they could have won one of the awards. When asked what caused them to think they could not win an award, they told story after story about the lack of support to do their jobs. They did not know what management's objectives or mission was. More significantly, they would have preferred better regular compensation than to see all that money spent on the lavish awards in the incentive program.

Have you noticed that you are now in Chapter Six – more than halfway through this book and my ROI process – and we have yet to talk about awards? Our case study client, the tool manufacturer in Southern California, was thinking the same thing right about this time.

*In exit interviews, departing employees talked about the incentive program. They even said they wished they could have won one of the awards. When asked what caused them to think they could not win an award, they told story after story about the lack of support to do their jobs.*

## Our California manufacturer: Not another survey!

The CEO of the tool company asked me if we were ready to roll on our incentive program. I could tell he was eager to see the outcome. The sooner he could see that, the better. I assured him that we were well on our way and I used our meeting for the next step in my ROI process.

We discussed the people side of the emerging incentive program – the sales staff and their sales support team. They were the foot soldiers who would carry out the plan that management had been developing. I suggested to the CEO that we needed to find out where production line employees thought management was headed.

He reacted with a "don't ask, don't tell" expression. "We just did a survey of employees," he said in frustration.

"But we now need a basic understanding of employee attitudes," I assured him, adding that we would do this with a simple, easy-to-complete employee survey. "What I am after is information that confirms management and the production line have a common understanding of where the company is heading – and whether we had all the right tools to build a sound incentive program."

The tool analogy worked really well, as you can imagine, and I did not even plan it that way!

We used informal sit-down interviews among the managers to gather their baseline information. The questions were ranked.

"On a scale of 1-5, with 5 being the highest score," I asked, "how much of an understanding do your employees have of overall company objectives?" Most initially responded with rankings of four or five, and that gave me a perfect opportunity. "So, if I were to ask your employees what the company seeks to achieve during the next three years," I asked, "they would be able to tell me?"

I knew what the answer would be. It's always the same: "Sure, the employees would know."

Were they in for a surprise.

"Well, maybe not specifically, but they know we want to grow and be competitive" was the common response. In other words, the employees had only a vague idea of what management expected …but not a clear idea. Why the need for a clear idea versus a vague idea, you ask? Well, wouldn't any employee of any company guess that the employer wants to grow the business and be competitive? After all, few employees would guess their company wants to march smartly into bankruptcy. Vague notions are just not helpful.

The human resources manager and I then distributed the survey questionnaire to the employees. We kept it to seven simple questions. The answers would tell us if both managers and employees were united on the same path with the right resources.

It would also reveal if employees believed they were fairly compensated. We received a variety of responses on compensation. Human resources handled a few remaining issues, working directly with the supervisors and their employees.

We were now satisfied we had reached a satisfactory baseline of understanding to proceed with an incentive program.

You may choose to use a survey questionnaire to gather baseline information. But the reliability of survey research rests on carefully constructed questions that do not gather confusing responses. A good example is the questionnaire your congressman sends you once a year.

## Now for your incentive program

Your ROI incentive program will target specific participants. To meet your program objectives, the participants must be motivated to achieve results beyond the norm.

What groups, job functions, or other participants could be targeted for incentives? Some prospects include:

- Sales staff
- Sales support
- Customer Service
- Engineering
- Operations
- Customers
- Dealers
- Retailers
- Distributors
- Major suppliers

For employees, the right information can be obtained from their immediate supervisors or their department managers. You can also use face-to-face meetings, personal interviews, or surveys to gather the needed profile information.

Such information can affect your impact analysis, the topic discussed in Chapter Four. But whereas Chapter Four urged you to interview the managers of departments outside the incentive program, we now urge you to assess the perceptions of the direct participants in your incentive program.

## Surveying individual participants

Incentive programs are often launched without first verifying that targeted participants are likely to be motivated and ready to participate. You must know that before you start an incentive program.

The resources section at the end of this chapter refers to a Maritz Research white paper that has several important recommendations.

• Surveys should measure employee engagement and commitment, not just employee satisfaction. What is employee engagement? It's the difference between an employee who may be content with compensation and benefits but may not be enthusiastic about going beyond the norm – as in an incentive program. You wouldn't want to start an incentive program if many employees would ignore it.

• All items in an employee survey should be actionable, meaning you can do something about the results.

• Make sure you know what employees want, which may require digging deeper so you can be certain a sufficient level of engagement exists to start an incentive program.

By surveying targeted participants about their work environment, you will gain valuable information that can fine-tune a successful ROI incentive program. Survey responses will provide a baseline for comparison.

Conduct a survey before you start your program so you can be certain they are ready to be motivated. Survey during the program to see how attitudes and perceptions may have changed. And, of course, survey after the program to compare progress and measure success.

A good survey technique is the five-point graded response, 5 meaning "strongly agree" and 1 meaning "strongly disagree." Writing survey questions is an art form. Don't hesitate to get assistance.

The following are subject areas that can be included in your survey:

## Compensation

"What are they thinking? Why don't they just give us the money and pay us what we're worth instead of waving all these trips and toasters at us! "

If that's what you employees think, put your incentive program on hold for a while. Something is wrong both with your compensation and your incentive program planning.

A real incentive program is intended to motivate employees to achieve beyond normal levels of performance. It's a challenge, and a challenge should be attractive. But an incentive program cannot work if it is perceived as compensation or is resented as compensation deserved.

To uncover perceptions, just ask how they feel about their current salary and benefits. Many companies' compensation plans vary with local costs of living, so a survey helps management to track those variations. The question I've used: "My salary/wage meets function, industry, and geographic norms."

You might say, "Oh, Dawson, of course the employees will say they are not paid enough, so what's the good of the survey?" Wrong. I am amazed how often such surveys reveal that employees are more concerned with work/life balance, working conditions, managerial issues and other factors more than they are concerned with compensation. More importantly, you are trying to compare management's perceptions of compensation with employee perceptions. If management answers "5" and employees, on average, grade compensation as "2" or "3," you have a compensation disagreement that will almost surely cripple any incentive program.

## Company goals

How well have your company's overall goals and objectives been communicated to your incentive program participants? Have the company's mission statement and goals been communicated to program participants?

It is not unusual for incentive program participants to be unaware of the company's unique selling proposition or its mission statement. Program participants must understand the company's strategy, mission statement, and goals before they can understand how the incentive objectives relate to the mission or goals. Do you need to reintroduce the company's strategy and mission statement?

## Company support

As indicated in Chapter Four, your ROI incentive program needs the cooperation of non-targeted departments. But targeted participants will decide to participate only if they foresee success for themselves. So survey them about how they perceive the levels of support currently provided by other departments.

## Geographic differences

Where are participants located? If your company has multiple locations and targeted participants are spread throughout, you must identify geographic differences. Such differences will prompt different perceptions, and they might affect the ability of local participants to qualify for awards.

Perceptions of other people's locales can be naïve and impractical. A sales professional who covers New York City by subway leads a different life from a colleague whose West Texas territory requires five overnights and a company car. One can carry lots of samples; the other cannot. An incentive to close sales for a new product in a territory that is chiefly commercial may not work for someone whose territory is the District of Columbia filled with slow-moving bureaucrats.

Some cities are restricting certain packaging and even foods, which makes it difficult for a sales representative to sell a new product with the wrong wrappers or content. Some hospitals are restricting the visits of pharmaceutical sales people, whereas their colleagues in other states may have no such worries.

## Age differences

What is the age range of the program participants? If two groups of participants vary greatly in age, the selection of incentive awards can be difficult. What appeals to a married, 50 year old may not command the attention of a 25-year old single person.

This is especially true of trip awards. The 20-something awardees are hot to trot on that beach property. But the 50-somethings can't take the trip because they have children in school. You would be surprised how often incentive managers choose trip awards without checking how the trip dates might conflict with the lives of participants.

Keep in mind one of the principles of incentive ROI: Choose awards that participants would not or could not obtain on their own.

## Skill levels

Depending upon your company's size and scope, you may have incentive program participants with varying skill levels. To motivate each individual and to provide all participants an equal opportunity for success, find out how they perceive their skill levels.

What type of industry related experience do participants have? What type of company experience do they have? Is it sufficient for them to meet the program objectives?

How well have participants been trained? How much training and support does your company provide? The key question is a simple one: Do they have the training to do their job well right now…before you through an incentive program at them? That's a question that demands an honest answer.

## Tools of the trade

Do participants have the tools to do the job? Tools come in many forms. Information regarding your competition is a tool. Marketing brochures are tools. Sales training is a tool.

Telephone skills, including how to handle upset customers, are tools. Do the participants have the computer productivity tools to manage information efficiently?

Having the tools is one element; knowing how to use them is another. Buying a great inventory and fulfillment system is a big investment, but buying to training to use it effectively is equally important. Are you sure your program participants know how to use them?

---

### The take-away

**Guiding principle:** An effective incentive program must start with a unified baseline of perceptions – participants' perceptions that mesh with management perceptions. Such baselines enable you to track the critical non-financial aspects of your results, and such information provides early warnings of where management and incentive participants' perceptions may be at odds.

**Solution:** Employees make a decision, consciously or unconsciously, to participate or not participate in an incentive program. The decision is based on their perceptions, regardless of whether those perceptions are accurate or inaccurate. Remember what Tom Peters said about perceptions. An employee decides, "Is this incentive program worth it to me?"

**Example:** Research supports this notion. Many researchers have shown that employees like quota-based incentive programs because of the obvious opportunity to make more money. Also, quota based incentives apparently increase an employee's perception of control.[7]

---

### How does your program measure up?

What data have you collected about participants' perceptions of past incentive program? If you haven't done so, you are not ready to launch an incentive program. How do the targeted participants perceive their compensation? Are you certain they are content? If they are not, they could resent the incentive program rather than strive to meet its objectives. Are you certain the likely participants have the tools to do their jobs right now, and do they know how to use them? What regional differences could make an incentive program unattainable for some participants? What differences among participants could make the incentive awards unappealing to some participants?

All such information formed a baseline for judging your incentive program's success. And all such data could change everything, from your objectives to your impact analysis to your rules structure and awards.

You now have some good data about your business and your targeted incentive program participants. Now it's time to figure out what your program costs will be and what should be purchased. That's budgeting, and that's Chapter Seven.

## End Notes

[1] Corporate Leadership Council (2004). Driving performance and retention through employee engagement. Reston, Virginia. Corporate Executive Board. www.clc.executiveboard.com.

[2] Condly, S. et al (2004, January). Motivation in the hospitality industry. Incentive Research Foundation (IRF). www.theirf.org.

[3] Oakley, J. (2004, August). Linking organizational characteristics to employee attitudes and behavior: A look at the downstream effects on market response and financial performance. Evanston, Illinois. Forum for People Performance Management and Measurement, Northwestern University.

[4] Sirota, D., Mischkind, L. & Melzer, M. (2005). The Enthusiastic Employee: How companies profit by giving workers what they want (Philadelphia: Wharton School Publishing); and Lambert, A. (2006). Employee Surveys: Good practices, trends, and developments (London: Corporate Research Forum).

[5] Zeithaml, V., Parasuraman, P., and Berry, L. (1990). Delivering Quality Service. New York: Free Press; p. 146.

[6] Holmes, P. (2001). Recognition vs. compensation. Selling Communications, Inc. and the Sales Marketing Network.

[7] Bandura, A. (1997), Self-Efficacy: The exercise of control. Worth Publishers.

# Chapter 7:

## Budget Planning: Everybody in the pool

> *"Never base your budget requests on realistic assumptions, as this could lead to a decrease in your funding."*
>
> — **Dilbert cartoonist Scott Adams**

Everyone in your organization has an opinion about your incentive program and budgets, including those who are not participants or program managers. Don't be annoyed; invite them into the discussion. Such discussions can help your incentive program budget become more accepted and credible.

In Chapter Four and Five, you learned the importance of reviewing the impact of internal and external influences of your program. My experience in incentive consulting has revealed that the larger the company, the lesser the support for the incentive program from other areas of the company. The same can be said of incentive program budgets.

### The Gist

**Starting with awards and then setting a budget is backwards. Your budget should consider more than just the cost of the awards. Accurately assembling all the financial data helps you to arrive at a true forecast of your potential for a best case, most likely case, and worst-case budget. Such an exercise will enable you to provide a true return on investment (ROI) picture for your incentive program. In this chapter you will see that this budget process does not require you to be a financial analyst.**

Creating a budget for an incentive program is fraught with misconceptions. Incentive program budgets are not about magic or creativity. The incentive budget should focus on one criterion only – your financial or quantitative objectives.

Here's the big question I ask every client: What would it take for you to create an incentive program and awards that your participants would really and truly perceive as a "could not, would not buy on my own" experience? I have yet to meet anyone who has worked through the budget process for an incentive program that responds to that question with anything other than "more money."

It never ceases to puzzle me. Why do these same incentive planners struggle to cram their program into a budget that seems to have been set by throwing darts at numbers? We must all reverse this backwards way of budgeting. It makes no logical sense. If you reverse this process, I will demonstrate for you and your company that incentive programs are a valuable management tool worthy of both the risk and rewards of the investment of budget dollars.

## A short success story...

A computer manufacturer targeted its value added resellers (VARs) with incentive programs. During the boom years, when funds were flowing freely into the high tech industry, these programs were well funded. The firm's VARs were eager to compete for a seat on a spectacular trip.

Then the high tech boom fizzled. The incentive budget was among the first items to come under scrutiny. The CFO was quick to remind everyone of his lack of fondness for the program. Faced with a dilemma – cut the budget or cut the program –the incentive program team wanted to show that their program worked.

First management examined past incentive programs and their influence on other department budgets. They were shocked that their incentive programs cost the company far more than they realized.

Armed with this new sensitivity for the financial ripple effect incentive programs had throughout the company, the team designed an incentive budget that included all revenue and cost centers. That process started by listing each of the financial categories they agreed would be measured throughout the program: revenue, cost of goods sold, gross margin, sales and marketing expenses, and net profit.

The budget projection then considered three scenarios: best-case budget, most-likely case, and worse-case budget. In each of these cases, the team projected what they thought would be the potential outcome above what they had established as their baseline starting point for each of the categories. Only after they crunched the numbers did they arrive at a revised incentive program budget.

|  | Last Year Actuals | Next Year Projected | Projected Best Case | Projected Most Likely | Projected Worst Case |
|---|---|---|---|---|---|
| Net Sales | $20,000,000 | $20,600,000 | $22,248,000 | $22,042,000 | $21,836,000 |
| Cost of Goods Sold | $13,900,000 | $14,214,000 | $14,238,720 | $14,327,300 | $14,411,760 |
| Gross Margin | $6,100,000 | $6,386,000 | $8,009,280 | $7,714,700 | $7,424,240 |
| S&M Expense | $5,800,000 | $5,768,000 | $5,784,480 | $5,730,920 | $5,895,720 |
| Net Income | $300,000 | $618,000 | $2,224,800 | $1,983,780 | $1,528,520 |

The CFO praised their efforts. He even began looking at the incentive program as an investment in growth rather than dismissing it as bloated cost. The following year, the incentive budget actually exceeded original projections and those of past years. The CFO was quick to observe the program's results also exceeded objectives – *during a time when the market was still depressed.*

The VARs that were involved in the incentive program were also amazed. They knew that times were tight, yet they noticed that the incentive program "value" had not diminished at all. This was an audience that was being hit, in a down market, with all types of incentives from competing manufacturers. But when the VARs compared those programs to what this company was offering, the differences were clear. The relationships that were cemented through this tough economic time created a huge advantage for this company once the markets started to come back.

## ... but how one program failed

A worldwide telecommunications company utilized incentive programs to motivate dealers around the world to sell both products and service contracts. The awards included both a luxury travel program and high-end merchandise. The incentive trip was an all-inclusive package. Participants and their guests were provided with luxury resort accommodations, all meals and amenities, sports activities, and transportation. Each year the firm's executive committee decided the budget for these awards.

The company continued to expand its dealer network and, as a result, the number of incentive participants increased as well. Everyone seemed optimistic.

But during one year's budgeting session, management was reviewing the numbers and questioning the large expenditure. They had retained an outside incentive provider and instructed them to revise the program proposals. Specifically, management wanted to reduce the budget per award qualifier *but without eliminating any of the features that had made this program such a success.*

While the incentive company was able to find some deals to help satisfy management's wishes, those same deals created budget issues in subsequent years. It became increasingly difficult to find the deals they needed for the favored destinations and desired trip dates. The only solution was to reduce the number of days for the award trip to accommodate the new budget restrictions.

But dealers saw this as a big de-motivator because of the time required just to travel to and from the destinations selected. Participant numbers dropped substantially. Eventually this once valued program was cancelled altogether and the sponsoring company found itself losing market share.

*But dealers saw this as a big de-motivator because of the time required just to travel to and from the destinations selected. Participant numbers dropped substantially.*

### What must come first

Don't dream of possible awards and then try to create a budget around them. Set the budget for your ROI incentive program before you select awards. Again, please note we haven't even discussed awards in this book yet.

The only criterion for incentive budget setting is financial, quantitative objectives.

To project your ROI incentive program budget to meet such objectives, start with a baseline of numbers and build from it. But you must use all the real costs. Your baseline is the present starting point for each quantitative objective.

It is very important that baseline numbers match the time period of the proposed new ROI incentive program. For example, if you are planning to run your program during the first quarter of the next year, your baseline numbers must come from your most recent first quarter. Your ROI incentive program budget will be measured on the incremental improvement from that baseline number.

When I am setting these baseline numbers for my clients, I ask three simple questions:

1. What did you do last year in revenue, cost of goods sold, and the other categories?

2. For these same categories, what are you projecting will happen this year – without an incentive program?

3. Did any one-time events occur in either the revenue or expense that could distort our projections for incremental improvements?

Gathering those answers makes a projection of incentive results more realistic. I then ask three more questions:

1. What do we think this program would do, in each area we have identified, if we absolutely hit it all right (best case)?

2. What would happen if we got "most" of it right (most likely case)?

3. What happens if we missed the mark (worst case)?

| | Last Year Actuals | Next Year Projected | Projected Best Case | Projected Most Likely | Projected Worst Case |
|---|---|---|---|---|---|
| Net Sales | $20,000,000 | $20,600,000 | $22,248,000 | $22,042,000 | $21,836,000 |
| Cost of Goods Sold | $13,900,000 | $14,214,000 | $14,238,720 | $14,327,300 | $14,411,760 |
| Gross Margin | $6,100,000 | $6,386,000 | $8,009,280 | $7,714,700 | $7,424,240 |
| S & M Expense | $5,800,000 | $5,768,000 | $5,784,480 | $5,730,920 | $5,895,720 |
| Net Income | $300,000 | $618,000 | $2,224,800 | $1,983,780 | $1,528,520 |

## A look at someone's incentive budget channel conflicts

Large companies operating in several marketing channels frequently deal with channel conflict. Let's take a look at how this played out at one very large company.

The head of one of the firm's channel marketing divisions asked me to help develop an incentive program that would demonstrate return on investment (ROI). When we arrived at the budgeting stage, I saw an immediate conflict: Although one executive signed all the payroll checks, the various channel departments all acted as if they were independent companies. Consequently, channel managers treated their promotional spending as competitive secrets. How could we have a realistic budget that would reflect all areas where revenue and expenses might change as a result of the incentive program?

Incentive budget forecasts are based on incremental improvements. In other words, "This is what we expect to happen as a direct result of the incentive program." Based on that premise, the incentive ROI budget process considers three elements.

First, we consider the prior incentive program time period (same time of the year, same group of individuals, and so on). Next we factor the budget projections without an incentive program. Finally, we project what could happen if our program creates an optimal change, above average, or only an average change.

So the firm's marketing team and I began preparing a budget for this one channel division. The vice president would approve the budget over all the company's channel marketing – *exactly the person I needed to direct a big message.* But we had little data from the other channels and their incentive program successes or failures. Our budget was a guess based on data from one division.

The team members asked me to join the meeting because my explanation of this budget might be helpful. The meeting would include all of the other (competing) channel managers – just the group I needed to drive home the point about incentive ROI.

Knowing exactly what would happen, I could hardly wait as the date approached.

What a meeting! It reminded me of a family of children circled around a kitchen table, all pleading their case for a bigger allowance.

Each channel manager gave a separate presentation. Each was well done with lots of marketing spin.

Then it was my group's turn. We had no animated movies. No PowerPoint® slides. All we had was a layout of the proposed incentive budget and a brief description of the incentive participants we were targeting. But one thing was distinct: We showed that we could implement our plan with a positive ROI.

At the completion of our simple presentation, most of the questions we received sounded like this:

- "What about the effect *my* marketing plan will have on that revenue growth?"

- "Some of that sales growth will be driven *by my department's advertising* to the *same audience,* so how will we be able to tell what prompted what?"

Once the conversation settled, I stood and said, "We're so happy to have all of you available to participate in this process. For the past six weeks, despite our best efforts, we have been unable to get you to provide us with any input to this plan."

Eyes began glancing left and right.

"We welcome your input," I graciously continued, "because our plan is based on providing a measurable ROI that includes all potential income and expense that can be attributed to this incentive program. But without your input, *our team will assume 100% credit for any incremental change that occurs."*

I swear to this day I heard a pin drop in the back of the room. Nary was a word uttered, but an eye or two twitched as I took my seat.

Then the vice president of all channel marketing stood up. "Well, it seems like we may have an opportunity to unite our efforts," he wisely observed, "and actually provide our executive management team with what they have been hounding me for. So, I am asking that we all join this interesting process and begin to measure, as Mr. Dawson points out, the true ROI of what we do. I think it is the only way to really prove our value to this company."

Don't worry when the budget process seems like kids crying for more allowance. Leverage the opportunity.

I told you in what you would get from this chapter that this does not require you to have a financial background. I meant it! The California manufacturer we have been following had the same concerns. Their management team was not at all involved in the company financials. Here is how that worked for them.

## Our California manufacturer: *"Oh no…not financial statements!"*

I can still see the smile on the faces of the management team when we assembled to discuss their incentive program budget. The operations manager turned to me and joked, "You mean we finally graduated from incentive ROI boot camp?"

Yes, they had made it through my basic training. It was indeed a learning experience for them.

They had really looked forward to this meeting. "It's time to look at the awards for the program," they were likely thinking.

But the excitement lessened when I unveiled what we were going to review for an incentive ROI budget. They reacted as though the afternoon would be buried in a deep analysis of spreadsheets, ratios, and financial statements to review.

It was anything but that. The work had already been done and there was no need to complicate this process. I made it easy to see and easy to use.

In this case, I asked management to examine a simple income statement that included categories for revenue, cost of goods sold, marketing and sales expenses, and net income. These were the areas to be measured and would determine the true outcome of the program.

Our projections brought about some spirited debate, as it should. As with everything at this point in ROI incentive planning, nothing is cast in stone and this discussion was no different. We covered each category with a "what if" mentality in mind.

The process I introduced here is one I highly recommend you use, especially if this is your first attempt at demonstrating ROI from your incentive program. Quite simply, you have to allow the management team to come to an agreement, within reason, on how much change you will attribute (both income and expense) to your incentive program? In this case, we did our homework, so any recommendations had to be supported by facts, not feelings.

Using the information we had gathered to date, the management team began to see the rationale behind all of the steps we had taken. They quickly saw they were making an investment in incremental changes, and those changes would be reflected in the final results of the incentive program.

ROI incentive planning is not about trying to fit a budget into a program. This is an investment decision, not an award purchase decision. It is all about investing in a desirable outcome and creating a flexible plan to affect that outcome.

The managers at the tool manufacturer became engaged in the ROI incentive planning and truly felt ownership in the outcome. They were satisfied, and it was really satisfying to me to see all this fall logically into place.

Based on the various "what if" cases we ran, the final outcome told us that our "worst case" ROI scenario would yield a better return than what was projected by the company for the year without an incentive program. That's right, after including all of the additional costs we have mentioned (including the cost of the incentive program) and adding the incremental revenue, the net result – worst case – was still an attractive investment opportunity to make.

## Establishing your baseline data

Baseline data reflects your company's past. The baseline is where you start to build an incentive program that delivers the results you would not otherwise see.

Make sure your baseline numbers account for everything, including any one-time events. Such events may have caused changes in revenue or expense that can affect incentive program outcomes. Accounting for such situations helps you to avoid inaccurate projections for incremental improvement.

Examples of one-time instances include:

- A large sale or loss of a sale
- Merger or acquisition
- Process improvement
- Capital purchase
- Market share or territory changes
- Large customer acquisition
- Loss of a large customer

## Re-checking you objectives

Once you have calculated an adjusted baseline and considered other factors that may influence the achievement of your objectives, examine historical performance trends for the last three years. Considering the adjusted baseline data, trend data, and potential future impacts, make certain your incentive program objectives are realistic and achievable.

The baseline information you first set is what your company could achieve *without* an incentive program. Your ROI incentive program budget will then reflect the added costs of the desired financial changes you seek with the incentive program.

The big question: What incremental revenues and expenses will occur as a result of your ROI incentive program?

## Determining your ROI incentive program costs

You have already reviewed potential changes in revenue or expense that may occur in other departments due to your proposed ROI incentive program. As you begin to prepare your ROI incentive program budget, you should include any of these forecasted changes, in revenue or expense, for each of these areas.

Now add the direct costs associated with your ROI incentive program. Such program costs will vary, depending on your communication needs and your program awards. It is best to determine your program costs based on a percentage of the projected incremental improvement.

Program costs associated with ROI incentive program are normally 30-40 % of the total net return. For example, if your goal is to increase sales by $1 million, and your profits on those sales are 10% percent (or $100,000), the cost of the program would typically be 30 to 40%, or $30,000 to $40,000.

Consider the best case, most likely case, and worst-case program results. Calculate the return on investment for each scenario. What is the total net return minus all indirect costs to other departments resulting of the incentive program? Divide that by the direct program costs, i.e. the cost of running and promoting your incentive program. The following simple fraction summarizes it all:

## Total net return MINUS program costs

### Direct incentive program costs

| | Last Year Actuals | Next Year Projected | Projected Best Case | Projected Most Likely | Projected Worst Case |
|---|---|---|---|---|---|
| Net Sales | $20,000,000 | $20,600,000 | $22,248,000 | $22,042,000 | $21,836,000 |
| Cost of Goods Sold | $13,900,000 | $14,214,000 | $14,238,720 | $14,327,300 | $14,411,760 |
| Gross Margin | $6,100,000 | $6,386,000 | $8,009,280 | $7,714,700 | $7,424,240 |
| S&M Expense | $5,800,000 | $5,768,000 | $5,784,480 | $5,730,920 | $5,895,720 |
| Net Income | $300,000 | $618,000 | $2,224,800 | $1,983,780 | $1,528,520 |

This ROI calculation will provide you with a number: 1.31, .36, or similar. To determine the real value of your ROI Incentive Program, convert this into a dollar value. For example, for each $1.00 invested in your program, your company will earn, say, $1.31 or $0.36.

Review your return on investment calculations:

- Are they "positive" in each scenario? If not, determine if this program is still worth the risk before proceeding.

- How do they measure up to other investments that your company has made in the past?

This investment should, at minimum, equal the return your company earns from its regular, non-incentive investments. In many cases, incentive program ROI is much higher, with returns of 100% to 200% not uncommon.

### The take-away

**Guiding principle:** Incentive programs are designed to create change in a company. The budgets for these programs should be tied to the projected financial benefit of making the change(s), including all incremental revenues and expenses. Thus, the incentive award budget should be based on what would motivate the target audience to make the desired change.

**Solution:** Establish incentive program budgets following a thorough review of all incremental revenues and expenses. Projections are based on historical trends, taking into account any one-time instances that may have influenced the trend period.

Simple math then measures the proposed incremental improvements against all incremental costs to calculate if the program will yield a satisfactory return on investment (ROI). That's followed by a financial risk analysis: How much money is at stake if this incentive does not prompt change? Monthly monitoring is then required to maintain a safe investment posture.

**Example:** The key to establishing a true baseline for your incentive projections is creating a level playing field. Delete factors that will make it difficult to evaluate the true impact of your incentive program. The baseline projection is your company's income and expenses *if there were no incentive program.*

First note any unexpected occurrences from the previous year. These are typically one-time instances – significant revenue or expenses that were not anticipated when the projections were cast. They could also be anticipated events but were planned as a one-time event. Or it could be a one-time event but, in reviewing your external environment (Chapter Five), you anticipate it might last longer.

Let's say your revenue was projected at $500,000 and your $250,000 expense projection included a one-time, non-recurring charge of $50,000. The year ends with revenue at $600,000 and expenses at $275,000. Your revenue includes $50,000 that can be attributed to one sale from a customer that switched their business from a competitor that closed their doors. This new customer might typically buy $20,000 a year from a business like yours, so you know this $50,000 sale was due to a one-time order. Your company has a net increase of $30,000 above what you should realistically project for this one-time sale.

Your company bought new software as a planned (or even unplanned) cost, knowing such a purchase was a one-time expense. It will not recur in the following year.

Take these one-time revenues and expenses out of your calculations before making your incremental projections for your incentive program. Based on your inter-department discussions about the changes in revenue and expense from other areas of the company (Chapter Four), you are now projecting any financial changes in the coming year related directly to your incentive program. So what the budgeting process does is to correct your projection before the incentive program starts to avoid any surprises or faulty estimates of the return on your incentive program investment.

**How does your program measure up?**

If you choose awards first and then budget for them, your incentive program is based on faulty and incomplete data…and you are budgeting backwards. If your incentive budget is always under attack from other departments, that conflict is a sure sign you need to listen to them. If the CFO rolls his or her eyes whenever you start talking incentives (read, bloated costs), then you need to educate the CFO to the new logic of ROI incentive planning. The CFO will start listening to you.

The budget is set, but how are you going to manage the incentive investment so it pays off for you? Chapter Eight will give you that insight!

# Chapter 8:

## Managing Your Incentive Investment Risk: Keeping your eye on the ball

> *"Educated risks are the key to success."*
> — **William Olsten, CEO, Olsten Services Corporation**

You now realize I've been leading you through a concept quite different from anything you have known about incentives. Incentives are an investment in change that should yield a return on your investment.

But any form of investment requires identifying risk and managing it. It's the same with incentive programs. Presuming you have tackled risk management in other aspects of your business or personal life, you may find familiar concepts in this chapter.

But allow me to offer a challenging claim …

Your incentive program investment can provide your company with the highest potential return on investment, with the lowest potential risk, compared to any other investment that your company could make.

That's a bold statement I have repeatedly made to many executive committees, groups of CEOs, and several incentive executive forums over the years. I love to compare incentive program risk and return with other investments companies make day in and day out, such as research and development (R&D). It does get their attention.

### The Gist

**Your incentive program will operate in an ever-changing environment. That means your investment will be changing as well. Don't get caught up into thinking that your budget is cast in stone. This chapter will show you how to manage your investment to match the ebbs and flows of your program.**

### A short success story…

A high tech company, specializing in secure electronic payment technologies, provided lavish incentive travel programs for their worldwide resellers each year. The chairman/CEO of the company was personally involved in the smallest details of these annual programs. This attention to detail came as a natural extension of how this CEO ran his company.

Faced with new technology requirements every year, he knew how to establish budgets that would be flexible enough to meet changes in market demands. He managed the incentive budget in much the same fashion. Rather than establishing a budget and just tracking expenditures, he reviewed monthly where incentive participants were in relation to their incentive objective. This enabled him to fine-tune his projection of the final qualifying audience.

This constant investment review allowed the company to reduce program communication costs after four months by varying the communications sent to participants at the start of the program. Those participants who were projected to earn the trip continued to receive customized promotional communications from the destination resort. Those who were projected to fall short of earning a trip received encouraging and motivating communications that reflected their incremental improvements toward reaching the objectives.

In addition to these changes in communications cost, the company was also able to reduce the overall expenses for accommodations, ground transportation and special venue events that were all planned as a part of the incentive award. The various incentive program suppliers, such as the hotels, appreciated early notification of changes so they could avoid being burdened with financial losses for their businesses. Those relationships proved valuable for future arrangements with this company.

## ... but how one program failed

A national retail department store chain provided top-performing store managers with an incentive trip for both themselves and a guest. The marketing vice president was a big believer in incentives and had successfully used various forms of incentives to push store sales, even during traditionally slow seasons.

A key ingredient this VP used was something that had worked well for him when he was in a sales position years before. The incentive program communications were always delivered to the home address. This was intended to gain the attention and support of the store manager's spouse or significant other.

The VP was facing a weak sales projection for the coming year. He knew he had to pull out all of the creative stops to rally his store management team to reach their objectives. Being a true networking executive, this VP attended an incentive workshop at a major trade show and came away with some ideas about program communications that he thought would motivate his managers.

The communications began flowing to the homes of the targeted participants. Each month the communication piece added more details about the program, the fun experiences they would have, and the parties they would attend. Every piece included four-color photos of the resort, its sandy beaches, and happy couples sipping from drinks with those colorful umbrellas. The resort's general manager even sent personalized coconut to the homes.

The communications certainly did get attention. The excitement was electric.

But during the fifth month of the promotions, nearly the end of the seven-month incentive program, the VP was dismayed to receive requests from several store managers to stop sending promotional mailings to their home.

What could have been a problem with all those great scenes? They were all so enticing.

These store managers certainly wanted to meet the goals and earn the trip, but they had encountered situations beyond their control that would not allow them to qualify. Yet, their spouses or significant others were still pushing them to qualify. Each mailing added a bit of tension at home. That wasn't all. The VP came under fire from the CEO when the costs for these great fantasy-rich mailings exceeded the projected budget by 35% while the sales remained relatively flat.

## Short and long term investment strategies

The key to managing your incentive investment is no different than managing investments you make in retirement plans, college funds for your children, or even investments in hard assets for your business.

This is not about gambling where you hope to place a small bet and win the jackpot. Rather, this is all about building your incentive investment portfolio. Consider how your risk in the program will be managed because someone in your organization will eventually ask that question.

Let's get back to our case study. I will show you how that team constructed its incentive investment strategy.

## Our California manufacturer: The investment club meets

By the time we reached this stage, I was no longer working with a group of managers. It was as if I was working with one person. They were working in unison. They knew the outcome was strictly based on how well "we" managed this program as an investment.

Most incentive programs never reach such unity.

Our investment discussion started with the topic of risk and return. I explained that the only way for this incentive program to succeed was to have the targeted participants as engaged as we were. That's a function of communication. We must promote the program to them and, more importantly, how they could each earn the awards.

The sales manager had led most of our previous discussions. But this stage started with the marketing manager. Without prompting from me, he led us in a quick review of the various communication tactics that would work best. He followed that with some insights about how those tactics could be crafted and his estimate of the audience size.

His comments were a perfect lead-in for me.

Working from our incentive ROI budget, we agreed that the communications portion of the program should be treated as an investment. This group came up with a promotions budget that was 20% of the overall incentive program budget. We then plotted our monthly communication budget expenditures.

- Announcement communication – month #1: 30% of the total communication budget
- Monthly communications for months #2-3: 20% of the total communications budget
- Monthly communications for months #4-5: 30% of the communications budget
- Monthly communications for months # 6-7: 20% of the communications budget

Several factors led the management team to this budget allocation. First we discussed our risk. Despite our best efforts and all of the hard work we did to get this far, there is always a chance that the incentive program may not work as we thought it might. Hence, your investment risk is the money you spend to motivate your incentive participants to accept your program and, by doing so, create the incremental benefits you have projected.

Our team agreed it was a good risk to invest in the announcement communication that would go to the entire targeted audience we were trying to motivate. The team also agreed that follow-up in months two and three would be needed before we could judge just how many of our projected incentive participants would be engaged in the program.

This was an important stage of this program. The management team now understood that we were committed to spending 50% of the communication budget, no matter what the program did in terms of incremental improvement. We were fortunate to have the information needed to decide that.

A three-month target was drawn. If we determined by then that the program was moving toward our objectives and we could determine that we would earn a return on our investment, we would continue the program to the next stage. If things were falling behind and we were not achieving optimal results, we could re-evaluate the program and perhaps make changes and modify the budget accordingly. In other words, we always would have the opportunity to manage our program investment at an acceptable risk level.

At the end of this stage in the ROI process, the issue of investment versus risk was clear. In the worst case, we had agreed to invest up to 50% of the total communications budget, and that was so we could achieve an ROI that far exceeded that investment if this program worked according to plan.

Now it was time to present this investment opportunity to the executive board of the company. To my surprise, the management team asked me if I would join them as they presented the program to their executives. I was thrilled and couldn't wait for the opportunity to see the plan unfold.

The presentation went well. It simply compared this investment to other investments the company had made over the years. The comparison showed that the incentive program would yield the highest potential return with the lowest potential risk. That comparison is quite typical for the incentive ROI programs that I have done.

The executive board was truly excited to see this all play out. Several of the outside directors asked me to visit with them to see if this ROI stuff would work in their business. I told them what I tell every executive who sees this for the first time. "It is not a question of if this will work for you. The question is how well it will work for you."

## Evaluating your incentive risk

This part of the incentive ROI process is quite simple to understand and to explain to your management team. We all understand that an incentive program cannot be successful unless it excites the incentive audience and motivates them to take the actions you desire. That requires communicating to targeted participants what you want them to do, when you want them to do it, and how they will benefit by doing so.

Sound simple enough? It is this aspect of your incentive program – the communications budget – that determines your risk in the total program investment.

Let's assume that you have a total incentive audience of 1,000 people. Let's also assume that your incentive program, from start to finish, will run for seven months. Your budget has been set. Now you need to allocate the monthly costs, i.e. how that budget will be invested. Notice that I said invested, not spent.

Allocation of your communication budget is a good place to start. This is the budget that will be used to create all of the promotional messages designed to motivate your incentive audience to achieve their objectives. These communications will also keep participants informed of where they stand in the incentive program.

You already realize that not all 1,000 people will earn the incentive award. Some won't even try. If your model says all targeted participants will earn an award, stop now. Recast that projection. You should not project that kind of result from an incentive program.

In Chapter Nine on program rules we will focus on how to create a level playing field for your incentive participants and maintain your investment strategy.

To start your program promotion, however, you will be announcing your program (including the rules) to all 1,000-targeted participants. After that start, your communications, and hence your budget, should be monitored and adjusted to reflect how individual participants are progressing toward their incentive objective.

The promotion budget should be seen as a risk to your incentive investment because these are funds that must be spent to launch a successful incentive program. But that does not mean you need to risk your entire communication budget. As with any investment, you track your returns and make sure your money is used where it will be most effective.

Specifically, managing the risk of your communications budget means tracking how well your incentive audience is doing as they move from your baseline towards your incentive objective. I recommend a communications budget based upon the percentage of the total budget the client is willing to risk as the incentive program unfolds. The total budget falls into four categories:

**Phase One:** 25% of the total budget should be allocated for what I call the start-up phase of the program. This rollout phase will include promotional communications to your entire incentive audience.

**Phase Two:** 10-15% of the total budget is what should be allocated for the second phase of the program. For a seven-month program, this point is about the fourth month. You are more than halfway through and you have allocated about 40% of your communication budget.

At this stage, you should be able to identify how each participant is progressing toward the objective. Potential awards have motivated them for four months to reach their objective. If you identify participants who are now more than halfway through the program and have achieved only 40% of their objective, decide if it's realistic that they will reach 100% with only three months remaining. Personal promotions to them are not a sound investment.

**Phase Three:** 20-25% of the total budget will now be used to reach those incentive participants who you have determined may be within reach as well as those who just have to stretch a bit.

**Phase Four:** 30-35% of your budget will be allocated to wrap up your program. That includes giving participants a glimpse of what they have accomplished. For those who almost made it, these communications recognize them for trying hard so they are motivated to participate in the next incentive program.

In summary, your risked money is the first few months of that promotion budget. You look at your overall budget – best-case, most-likely case, and worse-case versions. If the projected return is acceptable, even at the worse case budget, then you can comfortably proceed with the incentive program.

You are now committed and the program has started. You need to promote the program to the participants. It will take at least two to three months to determine how well the incentive is being received. That expenditure of the promotion budget should be considered "at risk." If the program falls flat after three months, and you opt to cancel it, you are still out that budget money. But it's better to stop the program when early indicators show it is failing than to run up more cost.

Following this risk management strategy will help you to accomplish several tasks with your incentive program:

First, you will now be managing the financial risk the incentive program poses for your company. Essentially your risk is somewhere between phase one and phase two of the program rollout, or approximately 35-40% of your total communications budget.

Secondly, you will be tracking how your incentive audience is responding to the program. We all would love to believe that such elaborate incentive pre-planning would automatically produce the right program that will work for 100% of the targeted audience.

But that simply won't happen. Despite your best efforts, unforeseen events can happen. Some participants will never be motivated. People are people.

As you review your program, however, those people, be they individuals within a group or a whole group or region, will become conspicuous. Such a review helps you decide how to change your investment strategy for the next incentive program.

I've seen it work.

A national food distributor gave me one of the best examples of how this process can create more than just a monetary return for a business. The company conducted an annual incentive trip for their regional sales teams. These teams were spread across the country. Every year they competed for this coveted trip.

We ran the numbers. The vice president of sales then noted that the region most on-track to earn the award included a long-time employee who had barely moved towards his objective during the first four months of the program. This trend was quite easy to spot. All those around him, with the same type of objective, demographic profile, and market conditions, were performing well. The VP sensed something was amiss and decided to pay a personal visit to this employee.

The visit was revealing. The salesman's lag was due to serious personal issues. He was going through a painful divorce and had turned to drugs and alcohol to help him cope.

When I learned of the situation, I was horrified that bringing this trend to the attention of the VP might get the man fired at the worse possible time in his life. But my fear was short lived. The company did not fire this individual. Instead, they placed him into a treatment program and helped him sort out his divorce through counseling with his wife.

The VP of sales later told me that the company recognized that he was a valuable employee and, frankly, without the incentive program tracking, this situation could have gone unnoticed and a good salesman could have been lost forever.

It's all business, right? But this one sad story with a happy ending stayed with me for months. I had learned of a very human benefit of my incentive ROI concept.

That is why managing your incentive risk is so important. But if you follow the advice in this book, you will minimize the risk and maximize the chances your incentive program will succeed.

Can you say that about how you have managed your incentive programs up to now?

## Your incentive vendors and suppliers

Any incentive program involves outside vendors. They have committed time and effort and, in most cases, physical awards such as merchandise, flights, and rooms for your program. Such suppliers are another important component to managing your incentive investment.

It is to your advantage that they see themselves as your incentive partner. More so, you want them happy. Happy, cooperative vendors and suppliers are much easier to manage than those who have suffered the bad business manners and miscommunications of others.

*Now he had another problem. First, those participants who truly qualified were upset that they qualified the hard way while others qualified with lesser effort. A survey of their attitudes bristled with resentment.*

As you manage your incentive investment and monitor responses and activity, you will often see that your program projection is changing. Keep your incentive partners informed. Specifically, I recommend you communicate with these partners at phase two so they can adjust their expectations of the final award group. This is especially true of any contracts you have signed for such things as flights and accommodations. Alert incentive partners prior to any key deposit dates or contract review dates.

If you don't keep incentive suppliers informed, you may well be charged with costs that steal any return on your incentive investment. Allow me to recall some horror stories for you.

A national retail clothing chain arranged for an incentive trip to Hawaii for their store managers. Management did an excellent job of forecasting the best time for the trip to avoid their stores' heaviest selling season. But management had to book rooms during the hotels' heaviest season. What's more, the resort played it safe by requesting a large deposit upfront and a final payment for the rooms 45 days prior to arrival.

Unfortunately, the clothing chain's vice president of store operations took his eye off of the calendar. Before he could determine how many qualifiers he would have, he was past the 45-day deadline.

Oh, how he pleaded. But despite his best efforts to get the hotel to reduce his room count for a smaller group size, he was now faced with 20 beautiful but surplus ocean view rooms. Rather than going to his management and seek a solution, he decided to lessen the qualifications so 20 extra people would qualify during the last weeks of the program.

Now he had another problem. First, those participants who truly qualified were upset that they qualified the hard way while others qualified with lesser effort. A survey of their attitudes bristled with resentment. Secondly, the overall ROI for the program dropped from a "most likely case" to below "worst case" budget.

While the operations VP thought he was taking care of the problem, he created two new ones. He had to explain the drop in anticipated ROI and deal with a longer-term morale problem for the credibility of future incentive programs.

But treating vendors as partners can have another outcome.

An electronics component distributor conducted an incentive program that projected 75 rooms at a Caribbean resort. The program performed better than expected. In the final months of the program, management predicted they would require at least 110 rooms. The resort managers were very interested in keeping this business, now and in the future, so they studied their inventory and managed to accommodate all 110 rooms.

One small problem arose: The original 75 rooms all had great ocean view. To accommodate the extra rooms, the resort managed to provide 10 additional ocean view rooms, but the rest were off the garden.

When everyone arrived and checked in, the incentive participants were confused about how room assignments were decided. After all, everyone wanted the ocean view. The company complained to resort managers. Their reply was understandable. "Had we been given advance notice, we would have been able to accommodate the entire group with ocean view rooms."

Travel arrangements are not the only issue. Incentive merchandise suppliers often encounter the same problem. An incentive program projection calls for X in redemptions and winds up projecting Y redemptions. Such a shortfall is especially difficult if the sponsoring company has insisted that the award merchandise, shown in the award catalog, be shipped immediately upon redemption. Stocking inventory costs money, and so do rush orders for new merchandise. Either way, you pay. Showing your incentive participants merchandise awards that they cannot redeem cost you money. It's all part of managing your program investment!

## Long term investment strategy

You are probably thinking this is a lot of work just to get through one incentive program. True, but it's also a trade-off. Do you want to gamble blindly or do you want to make a sound investment? As the opening of this chapter states, this process is about investing for both the short-term and the long-term.

In the short-term, you will minimize your incentive investment risk and maximize your incentive investment return. That's why I call it incentive ROI. But you will also build a foundation for long-term added value.

Think about the incentive audience that you reviewed during phase two of your program. These are the targeted participants you have determined are not going to meet the incentive objective this year. But they did show some incremental improvement in their efforts.

We call this the middle group. While they did not meet the goal, they likely funded your entire incentive budget with their extra efforts. Cultivate them. This is where your future award earners are coming from, depending on how you set up the next incentive program and its qualifying rules.

Now think about your incentive partners. Do you anticipate using them for future incentive programs? Are they likely to work more eagerly with you compared to another incentive planner who did not keep them informed of changes and then stuck them with unoccupied rooms or surplus merchandise? These partners are a valuable resource. Make them part of your incentive investment planning team at the outset and maintain that posture with them for all of your incentive programs.

### The take-away

**Guiding principle:** Managing the risk of your incentive program is a key to achieving your overall program objectives. Managing this risk also contributes greatly to your short and long–term success in areas that extend beyond the dollars and cents of your investment. Proper management of this risk will foster long term relationships with your key industry partners and demonstrate to them that you are seek a win-win for both them and you.

**Solution:** Treat your incentive suppliers as partners, not just vendors. Involve this group as soon as you determine you will be relying on them for the success of your program. Establish the key dates you both need for advance notice of any changes in your program. Your communications should reflect the individual standings of your incentive participants. Sending a "We'll see you there!" message to an incentive participant who cannot qualify at that point in your program is not very motivating.

**Example:** As you communicate the program to your incentive participants, include the contacts from all of your incentive suppliers in that communication. That includes providing the suppliers an update report. You will be surprised at the reaction you will get. Should you need to go back to those suppliers to arrange for changes, even after a key deadline, they will be easier to work with.

## How does your program measure up?

Look back on some of your recent incentive programs. How often did you actually consider any risk involved in starting the program? How many of those programs had some bumps along the way? But rather than manage those risks, you softened the qualifications of the program so the number of qualifiers made you look better. And let's be really honest: How many times have you called that key incentive supplier and asked them to bend the contract for a room block because you have come up short?

You have a budget in place and a plan for managing the investment in your incentive program. But how will you tell participants to follow the plan? How will they know what to do and when to do it? It's all about rules, and poorly written rules are what often kill incentive programs. Hang in there. Let's move to the rules of the game in Chapter Nine.

# Chapter 9:

## Creating a Rules Structure: Strategic design to improve both profit and cash flow results

*"You cannot put the same shoe on every foot."*
— First century philosopher Publilius Syrus

The rules structure for an incentive program can expand the potential for greater results. The three basic criteria for incentive rules are flexibility, ease of understanding, and fairness to all targeted participants. With those criteria in mind, you will now see how your rules structure can create positive short and long-term measurable results.

Research shows that quota-based incentives are far more effective than piece rate, tournament, or fixed-rate incentive programs.[1] But it is essential to gauge accurately where your incentive participants are on their personal hierarchy of needs, discussed in Chapter One and the Appendix. If your incentive participants believe they have been mistreated or short-changed, the research indicates that no award will inspire them unless trust is restored or they regain job satisfaction.[2]

### The Gist

**The rules of your incentive program can generate commitment from all areas of your company, including people or departments that may not be targets for the incentive awards. If you have followed the incentive ROI process so far, your new insights about your business can help you to design incentive program rules that create positive behaviors that can influence your final results.**

### A short success story ...

An automotive parts manufacturer had long sponsored an incentive program aimed at wholesale auto parts distribution centers. This program had always been well received and distributors were moving the manufacturer's key SKUs. Three year sales figures indicated incremental revenues were higher than pre-incentive years.

But a closer look also revealed account receivables had crept from a 45-day average to 62 days. Distributors were obviously purchasing the targeted SKUs to gain incentive credit, but were also delaying payment.

Consequently, the manufacturer recast its incentive program to include both sales and payment terms. New rules stated that distributors could not qualify for the incentive award unless they met both a sales and a payment term objective. The recast program both increased sales and reduced account receivables to a 49-day average.

### ... but how one program failed

A winery implemented a sales incentive program aimed at distributorship owners. The winery outlined for each owner specific sales targets based on case shipments of selected varietals. The program was a short-term success story: Almost 95% of the owners purchased the required cases of wine.

But three months into the program, sales of the targeted varietals dropped. The winery's sales representatives were concerned and did some checking. Buyers at the distributorships claimed no additional purchases were needed. The owners had purchased more than enough during the incentive program and those cases were still in inventory. While the incentive program successfully increased sales, all it really accomplished was to load up the sales chain and cause an over-supply of the product.

*But a closer look also revealed accounts receivable had crept from a 45-day average to 62 days. Distributors were obviously purchasing the targeted SKUs to gain incentive credit, but were also delaying payment.*

### Our California manufacturer: The rules drive the results

Whenever I begin to work with clients on program rules, I often see surprised looks on the faces of department heads whose staffs are not targeted by the incentives. They have never been asked to participate in the rules structure. While most incentive planners understand the basics of establishing rules – keep it simple, make it fair – they stop at those basics.

Don't make that mistake. Your rules structure can dramatically change your short-term and long-term results. The rules can also provide you with key insights into your company. See how our California manufacturer realized this.

The marketing manager was chomping at the bit to start the communications launch for their incentive program. But one part was still missing. It was time to assemble the management team again to begin to put program rules into place.

At first, I sensed reluctance from some of the managers who were asked to participate. They didn't believe they needed to meet about rules if their department was not included in earning awards. If they participated, I promised they would again see why this is not about one area of the company – it was about all of us together.

With a full management team assembled, I returned to our discussion about objectives. That drew some laughs and comments, such as "I knew when I wished for that objective that, in the end, increased sales would still be the top objective."

Many of the objectives they had listed – their wish list – were indeed valid areas for improvement. Some objectives on the wish list did not make it to the final list because they did not score high enough. But now was the time to work some of these objectives into the program rules, I told them, and they seemed eager to hear how.

We all had agreed a key objective would be increased sales, so that's where I started. I asked the finance manager about any concerns he had regarding incentives to the sales team to increase sales. He was anxious about any pressure his staff would endure as they tried to book sales each month in time for the points to be credited to the sales person.

We all agreed that timely crediting of sales was important to meeting our investment objective. But a solution to the pressure on the finance staff was to add a rule stating when closed sales had to be reported each month. We were trying to avoid having an avalanche of sales orders ready for posting the same time as end-of-month closing and the preparation of reports for the executive committee. Easily done.

Other concerns were handled similarly. Finance also wanted timely collection of receivables. To help meet that objective, which you probably now understand increases cash flow each month, we established point values for the payment of invoices within the normal terms required. Distributors who participated would actually earn points towards their incentive award just for doing what they should have (but were not) been doing all along – paying their bills.

Operations expressed concerns about the timing of orders received and the ship dates requested. Distributors habitually delayed their orders until mid-week and then requested fast turn-around so they could meet their customer delivery schedules. The operations manager had trouble trying to schedule his team around this tendency and feared additional volume would add more strain.

Once again, we used point values in the rules to change this behavior. Distributors who signed up for the company's "Flex-Ship Program" (a new term we invented just for this program that is now a standard for the company) would earn points towards their incentive award. Flex-Ship was merely a ship date window that allowed the operations team to create a more linear shipping schedule than the troublesome peak and valley impasse they had in place.

After providing some insight for these two incentive rules, I was pleasantly surprised to find myself out of much of the discussion. The management team took to this like fish to water. They knew now that they actually had tools (no pun intended) to construct an incentive program that could change behaviors and hit elsewhere besides the top revenue line.

The finished product exceeded the standard for creating rules. Easy to understand, easy to communicate, built in flexibility, and most of all, they provided a high degree of protection for this incentive investment.

I was delighted. And I knew in my soul this program was going to be featured in this book long before I began working on it.

## Creating productive rules for *your* incentive program

Properly developed incentive rules do more than just drive participation in your program. Sound rules also uncover information you would not get in any other way.

You will learn more about the products and services included in your incentive program as well as the process by which they are delivered to customers. You will learn more about your competitors and your economic and legislative environment.

The wonderful thing about incentive programs is that they can drive behaviors. While most programs focus on increasing revenue by changing sales behavior, uncovering new marketing intelligence is also valuable.

I was working with a beverage distributor that had the "perfect storm" for this opportunity. They were competing against three other companies for customers in a fierce market. We all have seen these situations. Any of us who have watched the auto or airline industry know what happens when The Big Three make a change to pricing. Everyone else follows the lead and we consumers wind up the winner.

Although this client's industry did not fit such a model, the same patterns occurred. The three companies were constantly trying to gain market share through discounts, price cuts, and even providing trips to larger customers.

When I got involved, the incentive program was already in place. A quick look at the rules told me this program was all about bringing in sales at any cost.

I made a rather bold suggestion that nearly cost me this relationship. It survives to this day, because the suggestion worked.

I told the company's management to reduce the incentive point values for new accounts and sales and add point values for competitor intelligence. Simply put, I wanted to have the sales team calling on those accounts that their company lost to the other two players. These were situations in which the sales person knew the deal was not going to happen. However, if they ventured meekly in these accounts and came back with reasons why they couldn't close the deals, they earned points in their incentive program.

Sound crazy? Think again.

At the conclusion of this program, the information assembled revealed a great deal about their market position. It also provided insights about each sales representative: Not all sales people chose to go back to lost customers and gather the information, so what does that tell you? The market intelligence provided frank and honest feedback about specific company policies –not products, but policies that made it difficult for customers to do business with them.

This company started to look at their entire sales process, not just pricing. They now viewed themselves through the eyes of their customers. It took more than a year to achieve that new vision, but today this company enjoys a loyal customer base. With that loyalty, this company no longer engages in the discount pricing wars of the past.

Most program participants know more about your business and its environment than they realize … or share. Rules can be used to award points to participants who bring new information regarding competitors and changes in your marketplace. Points can also be awarded to participants who offer new strategies to meet competitive challenges.

Your forecasts are based on the various economic regions across your company's marketplace. Your rules structure can award points to employees who uncover information about customers' business environments. This information will allow you to develop strategies to react to these changes and to act proactively within your marketplace.

But to encourage such sharing, you must understand your participants and the environment in which they operate. Once that understanding occurs, your incentive rules can be designed to motivate them to achieve above and beyond expected levels.

Your rules structure should be adaptable to changes that may occur in your company's markets during your incentive program. To create this rules structure, start with the information we have encouraged you to identify and gather in the preceding chapters. Such information can be used to quantify incentive program results and to document the factors that may have influenced these results.

For example, let's assume your incentive program objective is to reduce manufacturing processing time. But new government legislation requires additional cycle time to assure quality control. Such legislation could affect your incentive objective. Awareness of that possibility enables you to react sooner and a flexible rules structure enables you to make necessary changes.

This type of situation is common in most manufacturing environments. Manufacturers often suffer an internal struggle among production speed, quality and, of course, safety. Each is an important aspect of any manufacturing environment. But if your incentive program rules emphasize only one or two of these, you may be placing a burden on another.

For example, let's say your incentive program is based on production of a certain number of items. In addition, you include a rule that says these items must meet quality standards. You have covered two of your bases.

But that may not be enough. During your program's operation, you might find production times are on track and quality standards are being met, but safety incidents are increasing. You will need to address that trend before it takes away all of what you might gain. By simply adding a rule to your program about safety practices, you can focus attention on safety and help to mitigate or stop an accident trend.

## Program participant profile

If your incentive program targets participants of varied experience, skill levels, regions, or market conditions, your rules structure's point values should compensate for such differences. Unfortunately, I often see incentive rules that do not compensate for differences. For some reason incentive planners feel that a level playing field means everyone has to achieve the same to qualify.

For example, what if you have an incentive participant who has been in-territory for sometime and has closed just about the entire market share available for your company. He or she receives the incentive program announcement and reacts with frustration on a rule that specifies a 5% increase to qualify for the coveted trip to paradise. There isn't a 5% increase to be had.

These sales people have few choices. Veterans will always leave room for these "increases" in their territory by holding out sales until the incentive program begins. Those who have not yet figured out such a trick will simply give up unless a competitor goes bankrupt or a new piece of business falls from the sky. If you value such people and believe they should qualify for the award, you will change the requirements. Otherwise, these folks will do what they normally do and wait out the program.

Not the best way to create behavior change, is it?

So, how do you handle this situation? Simple. Provide such super performers with a chance to earn incentive points for maintaining their market share. How valuable is that to your company? What is the cost of losing customers and having to replace them? In the case of sales people who do hide sales until the qualifying period begins, you can change that bad habit with your program rules, too.

## Open-end and closed-ended ROI incentive programs

How should you start designing your incentive rules structure? You begin with the end in mind.

How many of your program participants do you think will earn the award? To estimate this figure, you must carefully consider which of three ROI incentive program structures best suits your objectives: closed-ended, open-ended, or a combination of the two.

Closed-ended ROI incentive programs begin with a predetermined percentage of award winners.

Examples include:

- The top 10% of target participants will earn the award
- The top 100 target participants will earn the award
- The top three participants from each region will earn the award

Closed-ended programs should be considered if your target audience is:

- At the same level of experience, skills, or other factors
- Motivated by competition with each other
- In a situation where the chance to earn a "spot" is more motivating than any other aspect of your program

Open-ended ROI incentive programs start with no predetermined number of award earners. However, open-ended programs do have predetermined levels of achievement for participants. Examples include:

- All participants that exceed target objective by more than 5%
- Any region that exceeds target objective by 3%
- All participants with 1500 points

Open-ended programs are better in cases where your program participants:

- Have various levels of skill sets
- Are spread over a wide marketplace
- Represent a large number of participants

Customized ROI incentive programs rules can be used for either open-ended or closed-ended programs and are used if you have considerable diversity among program participants. Examples include:

- Veteran employees and new hires with the same job function

- A long-range objective whose completion date extends beyond the incentive program period. Incremental steps to achieve this goal can be rewarded with program points.

- A mix of program participants (e.g. customers, dealers, employees) with different rules for each group

## Developing initial rules

Carefully review the initial rules you developed in phase one of the program. As a reminder, phase one is defining your company's business cycle flow followed by setting your incentive objectives. Rate each rule according to its level of difficulty on a scale from one to five with five the most difficult to achieve. Then rank each rule according to the value it would offer toward your overall incentive program objective and your business. Use the same one to five scale.

With both rankings, you can now create a combination of rules, some easy, some difficult. Doing so enables all participants to earn some points. Those who work harder will earn even more points. Save some rules to add as you review your program results during each subsequent phase of the program in case you are not achieving desirable results.

Our California Manufacturer is a good example of how this can be done. While we agreed a sales increase was to be a program objective, we did so with the understanding that a sales increase was going to impact several other areas of the company.

Within the rules of that program, we assigned points to each of three areas that the targeted distributors could earn. They could achieve points for achieving their stated sales objective, paying their bills on time, and signing up for the newly created flexible ship program.

The rules also spelled out the required number of points they had to earn for an incentive award. The distributor had to meet all three rules to earn enough award points. Just increasing sales would not do it.

We knew the distributors would not likely achieve all three objectives every month, so we provided other opportunities. For example, distributors could earn bonus points if their sales people enrolled in an on-line training program the manufacturer had promoted for years without success.

As the program unfolded, we added additional bonus point opportunities for sales of selected SKUs. This was a planned rules activity integrated into the program at a pre-determined time so that we could maximize participation through the end of the program.

As your program progresses and your environment changes, you may determine that your objectives are too hard for your audience. In such an event, you might consider adding bonus points for new activities in your program.

Adding new products to your incentive program and communicating that selling such products can earn bonus points can accomplish this. Gathering competitive intelligence is another such addition that can revitalize a program.

Planning for incentive program results, especially in a constantly changing environment, can be challenging. Remember, your objective is that program participants maintain a high level of interest.

Perform a "what if" review. Calculate the best possible outcome for your incentive program by adding all possible points together for a total score. Look at performance over the last three years for the same activity. Based on historical performance data, calculate a "most likely case" and a "worst case" outcome for your program. The average of this data is the "most likely" outcome.

*Face facts. Not everybody will earn an award, but you want everybody to feel like they should try.*

### Establishing ROI incentive program dates

Several dates should be set for your ROI incentive program: the qualifying time period, the award redemption time period, and the development time period.

Several considerations are important to selecting your qualifying time period. Ask yourself:

- Do you have baseline data for the time period that you are considering? To have an effective measure for each objective, you need to create such a benchmark.

- Are you sure the total time period is a reasonable time for participants to achieve the objectives? Review each of your objectives and compare the selected program time period to the results of the previous matching time period.

- Check your company calendar. Is this a good time period to conduct an incentive program? Are there any other scheduled events, either internally or externally, that would pose a conflict with your program dates? Remember that outside factors may have relevant dates involved.

When your program has been completed and you have determined the award recipients, allow time for the redemption of the awards. If your award involves an incentive travel program, the recipients will be taken out of the workplace for the travel dates. Some questions to consider:

- Is the time period allotted for the award redemption or trip an acceptable time for your best people to be distracted by their award?

- Will your redemption time period allow for a high profile recognition event for all participants?

- Does your redemption time period have a definite start and end date?

A properly developed and managed ROI incentive program will foster positive change throughout your company. But to plan and operate a program as a one-time event is not the best use of this management tool. The plans for your follow-up incentive program should be incorporated into your rules structure to initiate your next program.

When you reviewed all of the possible objectives for your incentive program at the start of this book, you had to make some choices to get that list down to no more than two or three objectives. That does not mean that those other beneficial objectives, if realized, need to be tossed away. They may be quite valid and more attainable in your next incentive program. Incorporate them as you review both the rules for your present program and your next program.

For example, let's say your program rules have covered the essentials for achieving great sales results and you have adjusted your rules by adding new products into the mix. But perhaps you have not yet introduced anything about market intelligence. Use that piece during the last phase of your program to help any lagging incentive participants qualify for your program. Such an addition could become a starting objective for the next program. With the sales objectives in place, you can now add this important piece to the program in the following year. In essence, you are now asking your sales team to meet a sales objective and, in addition, add to your market intelligence.

### The take-away

**Guiding principle:** The basics for designing a rules structure are constant. Rules should be easy to understand. Rules need to be flexible. Rules should reflect a level playing field where all of your participants feel they have an opportunity to earn an award. Having those basics in place will allow you to have an incentive program built for successful participation. But this book is about creating a program with a rules structure that creates positive changes in all areas of your business.

**Solution:** Incentive program rules should be based on a total review of the business cycle flow, the identified objectives, and a completed impact analysis. Remember that garden hose. Done realistically, the rules can then temper the incremental changes projected by the incentive program. Incentive programs are investments that can improve the bottom line and generate cash flow.

**Example:** Follow the results of your incentive program through your business cycle and ask this simple question: "What change will happen if we achieve our objectives?" Then ask, "Who will feel that change?" Those answers will tell you how your incentive program will create a surprise ripple effect on those not involved in the incentive program. Now, design the rules either to mitigate or eliminate any potential negative impact on that audience.

## How does your program measure up?

Do you develop rules over a quick sandwich with staff or management? If so, you need to start over or you may risk the entire program investment. Keep in mind what one sales manager once told me: "If you motivate sales people to attain a certain goal, chances are they will do it. It's in their blood." The case studies in the chapter should surely tell you that ill-conceived rules can deliver results, to be sure, but they may be the wrong results.

Your program rules will not be attainable for everyone. Thinking otherwise could prompt you to lessen the rules and turn your incentive program into annually expected additional compensation.

Rules can make or break the program. They need attention before you get to the awards... and that's the topic over which you have waited for during these past nine chapters. Congratulate yourself on your patience. We're finally there: Chapter Ten will address incentive awards.

## End Notes

[1] Bonner, et al (2000, March). A review of the effects of financial incentives on performance in laboratory tasks: Implications for management accounting. <u>Journal of Management Accounting.</u>

[2] Holmes, Philip (2001), Recognition vs. compensation. <u>Selling Communications, Inc.</u> and the Sales Marketing Network

# Chapter 10:

## Incentive Awards: Evaluating and prescribing what works

*"People don't change their behavior unless it makes a difference for them to do so."*

— Football star Fran Tarkenton, author of *"How to Motivate People: Team Strategy"*

When you picked up this book, you probably thought it would give you good leads for incentive awards. But by now you should realize why I held you off until Chapter Ten to talk about the awards.

I do admit that incentive awards are the driving force behind the incentive program. But this chapter will show you an aspect of incentive awards you hadn't previously considered.

Awards should be carefully selected. Participants will ponder the award package as they ask themselves, "Is this award worth doing what they are asking me to do?"

Employee perceptions are discussed in Chapter Six. Types of awards carry their own perceptions. A majority of 540 incentive executives surveyed in one study[1] agreed that merchandise and travel awards are remembered longer than cash awards. About 75% of respondents agreed, either mildly or strongly, that incentive program participants perceived cash payments as part of their compensation rather than as an incentive. You may recall that this serious conflict of perceptions is addressed in Chapter One.

### The Gist

**Awards cannot be chosen without first assembling a budget (Chapter Seven). Awards cannot be chosen without first gathering profiles of your targeted participants and what might motivate them. In this chapter, you will see how easily your incentive program can falter with ill-chosen awards. You will also learn what must be done to choose awards that motivate participants to do what you want them to do. As importantly, your targeted participants are not clones of each other. What motivates one may not motivate all.**

*Sales & Marketing Management* magazine interviewed a sales executive who had substantial experience with incentive programs for sales people: "It's very rarely about the money, even in sales, because if someone is good in sales, he is going to make money wherever he goes. The work atmosphere is the key to keeping people, and if people are happy where they are working, they tend to stay there."[2]

Another study of 235 sales managers indicated they preferred non-cash awards for reaching most qualitative objectives, such as improvements in the overall organization. But a slim majority of these managers preferred cash/variable pay for short-term, tangible goals such as motivating sales people to increase sales.[3]

But the Maritz organization, a leading incentive company, studied more than 1,000 employees and divided them into six categories of motivation depending on respondents' profiles. The study concluded that changing demographics in the workplace call for more varied award packages in incentive programs. The researchers urged companies not to keep the same program format every year.[4]

"Generally, companies that have been doing incentive trips for years keep to the same formula, which is a mistake," says Rodger Stotz, Maritz's vice president and managing consultant. "It's important to do the due diligence before planning a trip to understand the population you're trying to motivate – and not assume what they want. It's all about learning what *they* yearn for," he added.[5]

You may find some familiar faces among the Maritz categories:

**Freedom Yearners,** 17% of surveyed population, are motivated less by material awards and are more interested in flexibility in their hours and activities. A trip with constantly scheduled activities might not be enjoyed.

**Nesters** were 20% of the respondents. These folks don't want to be away from their family too long and seek workplace/life style balance. Travel awards don't motivate them. If travel is the award, Nesters prefer a trip to a nearby destination that their family can also enjoy. Nesters, too, like flexible schedules.

**Award Seekers** were 22% of the surveyed group. These people like cash awards but also seek trophy value. They tend to be younger and without family and thus do like to travel awards.

**Bottom Liners** were 19% percent of respondents. Cash is king with this group. Of all the six categories, Bottom Liners cared least about praise and trophy value and preferred cash bonuses or cumulative award points that could be redeemed.

**Praise Cravers,** about 16%, seek managerial and peer recognition for their good work more than any other kind of award.

**Upward Movers** were only 8%. These folks seek the status, such as mentoring other employees or private time with the management. Cash awards or job flexibility are not as appealing to Upward Movers.

An extensive study of non-cash incentives used in non-sales programs indicates that merchandise awards are used twice as often as travel awards, with travel and recognition awards equally popular.[6]

Lots of studies, lots of numbers. So allow me to summarize all this for you: You can't do the same thing every year, and you can't assume the same award equally motivates all targeted participants. This is especially true if your incentive program targets organizational issues, such as improving customer relations or health or accident/safety reduction.

## A short success story...

A major automotive manufacturer provided incentive programs to dealership owners. Overall, the programs were effective. But the manufacturer soon noticed the owners were passing the travel awards to relatives or managers rather than using the award themselves. Merchandise redemption was down from previous years, too. A survey found the answer: The awards no longer appealed to owners.

The manufacturer's incentive team went to work on improving the participation of dealership owners. The team designed a profile of the target audience. The profile indicated these owners could easily purchase, for themselves, the awards that had been offered in previous incentive programs. Remember the "could not, would not buy on their own" perception introduced earlier?

The planners retained new incentive awards that would be perceived as exclusive and of limited availability. These awards appealed to owners of big dealerships. But the awards were also an incentive to owners of mid-sized and small dealerships. They saw in the incentives the opportunity to earn a great award, but also boast that they were among the select and exclusive few who could qualify.

## ... but how one program failed

Every year a regional discount retailer conducted incentive programs for store managers. The managers, young and eager-to-please, saw the incentive awards as positive. The discounter's executive management team took pride in watching their managers enjoy receiving the incentive awards each year.

The retailer's incentive planner constantly looked for new and different awards to motivate the store managers. One year he seized the opportunity to secure space at a luxury resort. In another year, this property would have been outside his budget. Knowing he was lucky, he quickly sought management's approval.

The program was launched. Each month the store managers were excited by the appealing visuals and profiles about the special experience they would enjoy should they earn a spot on the trip. The program was rated a success because the number of managers who qualified was higher than the previous year.

Upon their arrival at the resort, however, winning managers felt out of place. This experience was certainly one they could never purchase on their own. But most of these young managers had never experienced such luxury and had no idea how to relax and enjoy it. Nonetheless, the store managers praised the trip award in later surveys.

The big problem occurred the next year. The company incentive planner was unable to secure a locale that was anything like the previous resort. But now the store managers expected the same spectacular experience. Their anticipation fizzled fast and post-trip surveys confirmed their disappointment.

## Awards: The tar baby of incentive programs

"Prove the value of incentives!" It's now common to hear that demand of both incentive industry leaders and the company executives and managers who sign the checks for their incentive programs. But no matter how often I hear that refrain, both of these audiences will get stuck on the awards early in the discussion of any incentive programs.

Why? Simple. Both audiences find awards easier to comprehend and discuss. Be honest with yourself. Which subject would you rather chat about, the numbers on your financial statement or that beach in Hawaii?

If you are serious about changing your incentive program to demonstrate the real value of it – a return on your investment – you must come to grips with this dilemma early on or the discussion will run away from you.

Resist the temptation to discuss awards before you have done your homework. If you do the preparation work outlined earlier in this book, be confident you will have an award offering that will suit your audience. With the Internet and companies like Amazon becoming an incentive merchandise fulfillment center, you need not worry about the award selection. The same is true of travel for either individuals or groups, to just about anywhere in the world.

It is much better to shop when you are confident your budget can actually afford what you consider for awards.

The management team from our California manufacturer case study could not wait to see where all of this was going to go. They were wide-eyed and eager when the awards meeting hit their schedule. Let's see what happened.

## Our California manufacturer: *What are we going to get…what are we going to get?*

This was the stage that many of the managers were waiting for. And why not? Over the years I have learned that everyone likes to talk about the awards for an incentive program. It's exciting for them.

I may be the only exception, as the preceding nine chapters revealed.

Working from a profile of the targeted audience, we began describing who the target participants were. How many men versus women? What age groups? How much income do they earn?

With those profiles, we outlined the kinds of awards that would deliver the highly perceived value we needed – that "could not, would not buy on their own" perception.

The big message for you – we outlined the awards without a concern for costs.

At this stage, we had a clearly defined incentive budget. We now knew that our incentive program could produce one of three outcomes – remember, best-case, worst-case, most-likely case – or some combination. We also knew that we were in control of that process. We were, after all, the investment advisory team and we had accumulated the knowledge and authority to say what the outcomes would be.

It was indeed tough to keep this group focused on possible awards without someone asking, "How much?" After a while, however, they began to see this stage of my ROI incentive planning much like the objectives setting stage.

They wanted to consider possible awards and see how each might impact the company's projections. Various award choices were possible, keeping in mind all of the factors that we had already learned about the audience and our potential for ROI with this program. Their attitude: What would we have to achieve to make this award a satisfactory investment?

The method I used with this group is one I have often used. They understood it; you can understand it.

When you are in the market for a new home or, even better, your children are at that stage, do you first find the home and then figure out how to pay for it? Or do you figure out how much house you can afford and then go looking for that house. The household budget is set, so now let's figure out what we can spend and still have enough to save for our future. The same idea applies to incentive awards.

At one point, the team members started to worry that they might not have enough budget to get that "would not, could not experience." So I answered, "Then we start over and see if we have built a budget that takes everything into perspective." I always get the same "Oh no …not all over" reaction to that comment.

But in all the years I have been consulting on incentive program, starting over has yet to happen. In this case, we simply forecasted and identified those who might earn awards and, by doing so, we came up with several scenarios. That's how it should work. If we achieved our "best case" scenario, sufficient budget funds were available to have more participants in the program. But that would also mean the incentive program would have generated a higher return. So our investment was intact.

The idea is simple: Identify the type of award that will motivate *that particular target audience* to achieve the incentive revenue and maintain your projected level of ROI.

> *East coast companies, particularly those based in New York City, think an outing to Florida is ideal. Never mind how humid Florida is, because New York gets humid, too. But west coast participants may see Florida as old, tired turf compared to a weekend in Santa Fe.*

### Mistakes in selecting awards

After years as an incentive consultant, I am amazed at the silly criteria some managers use to select awards. Many managers, suffering from tunnel vision, select awards because they think their selections are great without considering if all the participants – or any of them – would view the awards as something they could not and would not acquire on their own.

One company CEO was fascinated with old warplanes. An incentive company seized on that and cornered some fantastic replica models the CEO was certain would adorn the offices of every dealer in his channel. But those who won gave the model planes to their sons, leaving the dealers with nothing to remember except their hard work.

Choosing awards because someone else, such as a competitor, uses that award is a mistake. Selecting awards on the basis of price rather than perceived value in yet another mistake, as is choosing awards because of special distress or leverage pricing

But the common mistake in all such situations is choosing awards without first profiling your target incentive audience. For example, east coast companies, particularly those based in New York City, think an outing to Florida is ideal. Never mind how humid Florida is, because New York gets humid, too. But west coast participants may see Florida as old, tired turf compared to a weekend in Santa Fe.

Parents of school age children may be unable to take a week jaunt to anywhere and thus will not be motivated by such a trip unless it's a summer event their kids would also enjoy. Think family, not just targeted participants.

The same is true of merchandise. A twenty-something sales rep may be eager for a microwave or the latest computer game station as a monthly incentive, but not someone established in a household who isn't addicted to gaming. Would a Blackberry® or other PDA motivate a fifty-something sales representative used to his Day-Timer™ It might; it might not. Some older employees might never buy a Blackberry but would love to own one. By asking you might find out what appeals to each profile in your target audience.

## Cash versus non-monetary awards

Opinions differ widely in the debate about cash versus trips and other non-cash incentives. But one difference is hard to argue: trophy value. Cash is appreciated, but cash disappears. Incentive trips and tangible awards remain alive in office environments and conversation. They have staying power: they are visible, audible ... and memorable.

Status counts with everyone. Would you rather walk around the mall carrying a Sears bag or a Nordstrom bag?

Fun and creativity go a long way, too. A mortgage loan officer once interviewed said his favorite award was a month's use of a fully loaded Hummer and its high-profile parking space next to the bank president.[7] But would that award have any appeal for an environmental activist who constantly harps about renewable resources and the sin of internal combustion engines?

### The take-away

**Guiding principle:** First, calculate the incentive award investment required to meet your incentive projections and then choose the award – *not the other way around.* You may recall from Chapter Six the importance of perceptions. Perceived value is the number one criterion for selecting incentive awards. The second criterion for choosing an incentive award is the "could not, would not buy on their own" mindset. If they can buy it on their own, what's the point? Therefore, the needs of the targeted audience (e.g. internal sales representatives, store managers, distributors) should be carefully considered prior to selecting the award.

**Solution:** Incentive programs prompt behaviors throughout your company. How people are motivated and what motivates them entail a complex psychology that is well documented in business research. If all the guiding principles for planning incentive programs have been followed – the stuff of the earlier chapters – the selection process should be fairly easy to make.

**Example:** Your incentive participants are individuals. The award selection should match the individual as close as possible. This is your opportunity to think outside the box. Show your incentive participants that you have truly taken their individual needs into consideration when you selected the awards they could earn. If you do that, your program results will demonstrate a commitment unlike any you have ever seen before.

## How does your incentive program measure up?

These guidelines should leave you with *at least one profound thought*: Putting together an incentive award package isn't something that can be slapped together over a quick lunch with just your colleagues in sales and marketing. Remember that leaky hose referred to earlier in the book? If that's how you plan incentives, your investment in this book will serve you well.

You have your objectives. You have assessed the perceptions of needs of your targeted participants. The awards are chosen. Your incentive program is ready to launch. But you want to make sure you monitor how it unfolds and proceeds.

## End Notes

[1] Center for Concept Development, Ltd (2003, June). A study conducted among current users of merchandise and travel items for motivation/incentive applications. Incentive Central. www.incentivecentral.org. Prepared for Incentive Federation, Inc.

[2] Chang. J. (2004, October). Trophy Value. Sales & Marketing Management.

[3] Peltier, et al. (2005, December 23). Tactical tips from awards selection: Insights from managers. Evanston, Illinois. Forum for People Performance Management and Measurement (www.performanceforum.org), Northwestern University.

[4] Juergens, J. (2007, March 12). Match your employees to the right reward. New York, NY. Incentive magazine. Details of this October 2006 study are available from Maritz's director of consulting and strategic implementation.

[5] Juergens, ibid

[6] Center for Concept Development, ibid

[7] Chang, ibid

# Chapter 11:

# Tracking Results: Creating an incentive annuity

"Show me the money!" exclaimed Jerry Maguire. But if you want real incentive ROI, you had better exclaim, "Show me the data." Doing so may well lead to the money. Not doing so may well result in a repeat of all past mistakes, some of which will no doubt come back to haunt you.

If you have taken your incentive program this far, it's common to say, "I've done it! Now I can watch as my incentive program plays out and then bring that success back to my executive team and show them the money!"

Stop. Think of this incentive plan as your 401K.

When 401K investment plans first became popular, a friend at one of my client companies used to beam with excitement about her retirement account. She checked it daily to see how much she earned. I asked her if she was getting any professional advice about where to invest her money given that the market so easily fluctuated. She answered no, but my question did not damper her enthusiasm for her 401K.

Four months later I had an appointment with her CEO and found my friend quite distraught. The market had indeed taken one of its periodic corrections and she was seeing the change up close and personal.

Think about how the market changes in your business environment each day and month-to-month. With an incentive program in operation for an average of seven to nine months, do you want to take your eye off of it without being able to make your own market corrections? It's called incentive ROI for a good reason.

Read on…

## The Gist

**You cannot know if your incentive program yields a satisfactory return on your investment unless you track the numbers. You cannot judge the worth of your next incentive program unless you compare it to your current program. You cannot judge your current program without comparing it to your last program. Tracking progress and tracking costs are essential to the goal of incentive ROI. Otherwise, you are merely guessing. Are you ready to identify key tracking points?**

### A short success story...

A major American automobile manufacturer conducted incentive programs each year for the dealer network. The dealership owners would vie for an opportunity to earn passage on lavish trips loaded with spectacular experiences, such as attending the opening ceremony of the Olympics and even dining with the heads of state from participating countries.

During the days when manufacturing automobiles was a booming business in America, such incentive programs seemed so right and so easy to do. Honda, Toyota and Nissan had not yet slammed into Detroit's cars. But eventually these foreign players in the American auto market prompted changes throughout the industry.

The American culture was much different from the Japanese workforce. These new competitors studied how Americans worked and what motivated them. The Japanese auto executives could see things hidden plainly in sight, such as how our workers were closely managed rather than left to do a job with limited supervision. More importantly, they noticed how immediate gratification was much more important in America than reaching long-term success. Americans seem far less patient.

One Japanese auto manufacturer noticed that American auto company incentive programs stayed the same year after year, no matter what was happening in the industry or the economy. The competitor saw flaws in such consistency. They were right.

This Japanese company quickly introduced incentives to their own U.S. based workforce, but with a few changes. First, new incentive programs would be implemented only after senior management approved how the program would be measured and tracked each month. Each program had to include both short and long-range measurable goals. Rather than just piling one program on top of another and always trying to exceed last year's awards package, this new competitor looked ahead and designed their program to grow over time. They viewed the program as a growing tree.

The initial results were not apparent to their American counterparts. Many of those auto executives dismissed the Japanese program as a poor attempt at incentives because the awards were far less exotic. In the short term, the U.S. manufacturers actually saw some gains. But we all know what happened long-term and who is looking up at whom today?

## ...but how one program failed

A manufacturer and distributor of vitamins and personal care products conducted an annual incentive program for its independent resellers. The marketplace for these products had its ups and downs over the years, but the company stayed the course with few or no changes.

It soon became apparent the company had missed some changes in the marketplace that would soon affect the results of their annual incentive program. The sales model in this market had been the traditional distributor-to-retailer channel. But the consumer could now purchase directly from a distributor. In essence, the channel strategy known as network marketing crept into this manufacturer's world. Suddenly it was a whole new game in town.

The company attempted several dramatic changes in their annual incentive program to keep their distributors from dropping the product line. But, too late, this well-known manufacturer realized his sales channel was no longer going to be effective. While this company's management focused on trying to make the awards bigger and better to keep the attention of these distributors, the customers for these products were reaching out for more personal service and lower prices.

Their annual incentive program, once the standard by which their distributors were recognized, was cast off as a waste of money. No more President's Club Members.

Soon after the program was cancelled, the company was sold. Despite being sold to a group of network marketing industry veterans, the resurrected company soon lost its remaining luster. It was later resold to an international company. What was once a proud American manufacturer soon disappeared.

## Our California manufacturer: Moving up from last place to first!

The horses were now out of the gate. It was time to put the plan into operation. Some of the management team were ready just to sit back and watch and see what would happen, as if it was a race.

I gathered the team for yet another meeting. they were expecting it would be a celebration, as if we would smash a champagne bottle against the leg of the conference table. I had to break the news to them: Yes, we were indeed finished with our *program planning*, but we were merely at the start of our incentive investment plan.

We reviewed the concepts you have read so far in this book, such as economic and competitive environment and the changes already being made. Such a review is an important part of the incentive ROI process.

"How might you competitors react to our incentive program?" I asked. Suddenly three guesses came at me from different corners of the conference table. Those guesses were based on the managers' long experience with their competitors regarding price cuts, new product launches, and other events. Such experience set the tone for further tracking of the program.

A good analogy is to compare this stage of the incentive ROI process to managing a retirement plan. I asked if they would ever just put money into a plan and then ignore it until they retire? Nobody said "yes."

Their new program had been underway for just about two months when we met again. We analyzed three things:

- Where we were on target with our forecast?
- Where we were missing?
- More important, what adjustments seemed necessary?

This became a monthly event throughout the seven-month program. While we made only subtle changes in direction, those changes kept us on target for our investment goals.

Seven months later, we were in a good position to launch another incentive program for the following year. We also knew exactly how to focus that program and at whom.

What about the tool manufacturer's competitors? Stunned.

They were trying to figure out how this company came from last to first place in their category. And while they scratched their heads, our team was shoring up that new position and moving to create even more distance from any competition.

> *What about the tool manufacturer's competitors? Stunned. They were trying to figure out how this company came from last to first place in their category.*

### Tracking your incentive program: Your early warning system

When the time arrives to launch your ROI incentive program, it is also the right time to begin tracking the data. Tracking ensures success at the beginning, middle, and conclusion of your program.

Incentive programs have traditionally operated with an objective at the start followed by a review of the objective's success as the program ends. The problem with start/finish tracking is that many events, especially during longer programs, can change the level of achievement. You need to evaluate the program while it is in progress, not wait until it closes.

After all, you are trying to change something in the company or you wouldn't be implementing incentives. That implies tracking the program's effects on your operations.

Without cumulative tracking and a constant review process – during the program's operation – you cannot make corrections to minimize your financial risk or improve your results. Tracking enables you to see where you might fall short so you can take corrective action, such as adjusting your rules, before your program ends and potentially fails.

Simply put, incentive tracking gives you an early warning system that alerts you if your program objectives are at risk.

## Tracking critical dates of exposure

The first step is to track your marketing or promotional expenses and the deadlines to produce them. How will the program be promoted? Will you have a name, theme, or unique logo for your program? What types of materials or resources will you use to promote your program, such as videos, postcards, three-dimensional mailers, or a special intranet site? Identify activities and dates associated with these items

Examples of key activities may include:

- Date/lead-time by which your comptroller needs your check requests to pay vendors
- Program intranet or internet websites or links and their creation
- Copy/logo/artwork commencement and completion dates
- Merchandise and specialty advertising (logo imprint items)
- Postcard commencement and completion dates
- Mailing dates
- Payment due dates for suppliers and vendors.

The listed items require the talents of graphic arts designers and website designers. Your postal system has requirements for the dimensions of all surface mailings. Postal requirements constantly change, so don't have mailers produced without clearing the formats with postal authorities.

Make sure your incentive program colleagues note all such dates in their calendars. Note how many of these invoices will exceed your personal approval level, and then note your boss's itinerary so you are not caught without proper approvals at deadlines.

Next, look at the program awards, the key dates associated with the awards, and the projected value of total earned awards. Review all suppliers and vendor proposals, contracts, and other requirements. Develop a list of key activities associated with awards and their fulfillment.

Examples of key activities may include:

- Date/lead-time by which your comptroller needs your check requests to pay vendors
- Deposit/payment dates for suppliers
- Rooming list dates
- Cancellation dates
- Attrition dates, i.e. the cost of rooms or events cancelled after contract signing
- Final payment dates

Missing a rooming list or seat reservation date with a hotel or airline will result in losing reserved space. The seats and rooms will be sold to other customers. Hotels and airlines are in business to make money just as you are.

As with promotional deadlines and costs, your incentive program colleagues should note all important dates in their calendars. Such high-figure costs could well exceed your own approval level. Again, keep track of the boss.

## Establishing your ROI incentive program review

As you have already learned, your ROI incentive program will create changes beyond your objectives. During the program development phase, you reviewed how your incentive program might affect other parts of your company. But to track *actual* results, you will need to perform another review –a tracking review– while the program is in progress.

Perform your in-progress results review using the same format you used in the program conception stage. Your review should include:

- Management's view of how the month-to-date results compare to the goals management set

- A review of your competitive, economic, and regulatory environments

- Participants' view of the program to-date and their efforts and results

## Tracking your financial investment

Your operating budget is set. But as your program is running, regularly compare actual expenses to projected costs and program achievements. Any positive trends that are outpacing projections should be reviewed to ensure that the goals are not too easy to achieve and thus could dilute the overall value of your ROI incentive program.

This type of review should be performed at least twice during the program operational phase. But keep in mind important vendor commitment dates. Track as often as is necessary to capture critical data before you make each financial commitment. Specifically, allow yourself at least seven days prior to every key decision date.

Negative trends should be addressed immediately with appropriate actions or changes to rules. A negative trend is one that hinders your participants from reaching a goal, typically because of some unforeseen change in the market. An adjustment might be to add a bonus to help them earn additional points toward the goal.

Your incentive program may also show some surprising positive trends. Some participants may achieve their objectives faster than you projected. If that trend reveals valid achievement based on properly set objectives, consider bonus awards for either a percentage of goal (e.g. 115%) or a specific number. Such a modification can allow these high achievers to keep reaching higher. If you have been tracking your ROI, the cost of such extra awards should be adequately covered in your budget.

For each review conducted during your program's operation, note the date the review was performed. Such notations will help you fine-tune next season's incentive program.

## Your presentation to management

If you take the steps mentioned so far and you perform the operational review, you should have a clear picture of your program's operational status. You will also have the right information to present to management that shows them your incentive program will deliver real return on their investment.

Likewise, provide your program suppliers with the same updates. Suppliers can be an excellent source of support and information. They can help you achieve successful program results. After all, they want to talk about their participation in your success just as you do. If financial information is sensitive, use percentage estimates of completion.

## Concluding your program

At the conclusion of your incentive program, complete the operational results review. It should include employee surveys conducted prior to and during your program's operation.

Next, review the original participant profiles. Divide participants into three categories:

- Award earners,
- Those who achieved 60% to 99% of goal, and
- Those who achieved less than 60% of goal.

Review award earners carefully. Why were they successful? Examine where and how they earned their points. Were there any surprises about the award earners? For example, did any of your participants far exceed their objectives? Did any who you thought would be award earners fail to make it? How about those who seem to give up at the start? What did that tell you that you didn't know? Such surprises should be carefully investigated.

Note the award earners' competitive, economic, and legislative environments. Did any unanticipated changes occur in their environments and how did these changes affect these participants? Make notes of all these items for your future incentive program file.

Next examine the middle category of participants who achieved only 60 to 99%. Where and how did they earn their points? What were their competitive, economic and legislative environments? Did any unanticipated changes occur in their environments and how did such changes affect these participants? How did they respond?

Compare the results from this group to the results from the award-earners group. Note what productive changes should be made for future incentive programs. This middle group should be carefully managed after the program ends. Develop a separate strategy that will help them succeed in the next incentive program.

Consider these adjustments:

- Give credit towards next year's program for achievements that missed deadlines (e.g., fast-start credit for next year)

- Identify specific areas (e.g., training, new customer acquisition) where bonus points can be earned prior to the next incentive program's launch

- Initiate group discussion regarding "best practices" of award-earners

- Conduct one-to-one personal reviews with members of middle category and management

Lastly, examine the last category of participants who did not exceed 60%. Use the same guidelines outlined for the top two groups. Identify any specific circumstances or issues that could have prevented these participants from earning awards. Some factors may be their environments; some might be personal.

Why weren't they successful? Was one of the failing participants a complete surprise to all of you – someone no one every thought would miss his or her goals? If so, what may have prevented success? Did personal distractions arise? A valuable person who has succeeded before might need help in the next incentive program.

Make notes of what you learned about this group for your future incentive program file. Their objectives for the next incentive program should be carefully reviewed to ensure that the rules structure creates a level playing field for them.

Suggestions include:

- Additional training
- Marketing support in new/expanding territory
- One-to-one management counseling

The information you have collected can now be used to establish objectives and a rules structure for future programs. Based on a review of all three groups, you should be able to determine the award-earners for your next incentive program. By evaluating final results and determining what made people successful – and why some were not – you can ensure the success of your next incentive program.

Don't dismiss the non-performers as a bunch of losers. Why?

Allow me to share a story of what one CEO did at an awards banquet that still vibrates uneasily in my mind. It's a textbook case of how not to treat people who don't make goal. After all, you are reading this book because employee motivation and incentives are important to you.

### How not to run an awards banquet

I had the opportunity to speak before an audience of sales managers for a nationwide retailer a few years back. I met the CEO some years prior. He wanted me to speak to his team at their annual sales meeting about the true value of incentive programs.

The dinner was electric with anticipation. Spouses were eager for the award announcements. Shortly after my talk, the CEO walked up to the podium. You could hear a pin drop.

"Ok, it's the time we've all waited for," he announced as people perked up in their chairs. "I will now read out the names of our annual sales incentive trip award winners. I have your plane tickets right here. As I read your name, come up and get that ticket you worked so hard for."

One by one, he read the names with flourish. Some excited people ran to the stage to get their tickets. After all of the tickets were handed out, the CEO asked for a round of applause for all the people now standing on the stage, tickets in hand, beaming with smiles.

After the applause died down, the CEO stepped back up to the podium. I was expected a simple, "Thank you and good evening."

Not so.

"Those are our winners," he said sternly. "The rest of you are not winners. So I suggest you head out of here and try to figure out how you can be up here next year."

With that, the assembled diners rose and left, some still smiling, but many left downcast and dejected.

I was shocked. In all my years, I had never heard anything so harsh. The CEO approached me after the room emptied and appeared quite proud of what he had done. Rather than debate the issue – I was still swallowing – I asked, "Had any of the others come close?" "Were there any hopefuls that perhaps needed just one more sale to earn a ticket?"

"Don't know, don't care," he replied tartly. "I asked only for the winners' results. Why bother with those who did not make it. My eyes are on the people who carry the ball, not those who can't pick it up."

Why bother indeed!

Knowing which participants have achieved success and have earned the incentive awards is essential information. These individuals will receive lots of attention and well-deserved congratulations from their managers, co-workers, family and friends. But equally important is identifying the participants who did not make it. Were they provided with every opportunity along the way to achieve their objectives?

### The take-away

**Guiding principle:** You cannot be confident your incentive program will deliver a return on your investment unless you monitor and measure how your program progresses from start to finish … and all along the program's operation. Only then can you compare the data to the benchmarks set and to the results of the preceding incentive program.

**Solution:** In one word, vigilance. Your incentive program is much like any investment you manage. Things change. If you ignore your investment, you may get lucky and come out even. Chances are, however, you will come out less than even and it's highly unlikely you will achieve over-the-top results.

**Example:** Monitor the changes your incentive program prompts. Also monitor your initial risk investment, the communications budget. Allocate this budget to the progress your incentive participants make toward their objectives. Track the results of your participants with an eye on both this year's program and their potential qualification for future incentive programs. Read into what your incentive participants are telling you by how they react to making the changes your incentive program seeks. Act on that. Lastly, be mindful that your incentive program is an investment your company is making. But so have all of your incentive suppliers. Don't leave them out of your monitoring process. Incentive ROI is a team sport!

## How does your incentive program measure up?

Have you ever launched an incentive program and then sat back and waited to the end of the program to check results? If you have, it is entirely possible the program costs you as much as it earned you. That's not a percentage that makes for a successful business, so why accept the same percentage for an incentive program?

But you can take simple, logical steps to ensure success. Tracking does that for you. It's all about setting a new standard for an incentive program, a standard that leads to long-term improvements rather than short-term spurts.

## We come to the end of the process

That's it, folks. Your plane is landing. Or, your vacation is about over. Maybe it's Monday morning and you are heading into another meeting about sales and forecasts and…well… that upcoming incentive program.

You now know more about incentives than anyone else in the room. You are now the expert. Are you prepared to set a new tone?

# Appendix 1

## Helpful resources for incentive programs

**The Business Group, Inc.** www.businessgroupinc.com is a website for a company founded by Bob Dawson, this book's principal author. You will find several Incentive ROI Calculators™ to run the numbers on your incentive program and many more incentive industry resources here.

**The Incentive Research Foundation** (IRF) www.theirf.org The Incentive Research Foundation funds and promotes research to advance the science and enhance the awareness and appropriate application of motivation and incentives in business and industry globally. The goal is to increase the understanding, effective use and resultant benefits of incentives to businesses that currently use incentives and others interested in improved performance.

**The Society of Incentive and Travel Executives** (SITE) www.site-intl.org is "the only international, not-for-profit, professional association devoted to the pursuit of excellence in incentives…SITE provides educational seminars and information services to those who design, develop, promote, sell, administer, and operate motivational programs as an incentive to increase productivity in business. Currently SITE has over 2,100 members in 87 countries, with 35 local and regional chapters. Members represent corporate executives, incentive companies, destination management companies, travel & event planners, official tourist organizations, transportation companies, hotels and resorts, cruise lines, trade publications, and supporting organizations such as restaurants and visitors attractions. SITE sponsors the Certified Incentive Travel Executive (CITE) continuing education program that uses my materials for training.

**American Productivity & Quality Center** (APQC) www.apqc.org The American Productivity & Quality Center provides products and services to help organizations discover and implement best practices for obtaining measurable results.

**World at Work** www.worldatwork.org World at Work is a non-profit association dedicated to knowledge leadership in compensation, benefits and total rewards.

**Incentive Marketing Association** (IMA) www.incentivemarketing.org The Incentive Marketing Association leads incentive professionals and the corporate community as the premier educator and information source in the incentive marketplace.

**Incentive Central** www.incentivecentral.org Incentive Central provides planners with up-to-date, objective information to motivate people. Features include authoritative research, resources, and how-to information designed to help organizations achieve measurable business results.

**The International Society for Performance Improvement** (ISPI) **www.ispi.org** is the leading international association dedicated to improving productivity and performance in the workplace. ISPI represents more than 10,000 international and chapter members throughout the United States, Canada, and 40 other countries. ISPI's mission is to develop and recognize the proficiency of our members and advocate the use of Human Performance Technology. Assembling an Annual Conference & Expo and other educational events like the Institute, publishing books and periodicals, and supporting research are some of the ways ISPI works toward achieving this mission.

*Incentive* **magazine** www.incentivemag.com published monthly, focuses on all the issues surrounding the planning and implementation of incentive and motivation programs. Incentive is a controlled-circulation publication, which means subscription if free to those who are qualified incentive managers.

**The Motivation Show** www.themotivation.com the largest incentive exhibition and symposium, meets each September. 7,500 buyers and 6,000 exhibitors from more than 1,900 exhibiting companies come together to exchange ideas and learn what's working.

**EcoTrends®** is a monthly report published by The Institute for Trend Research www.ecotrends.org Speaking for themselves, "The Executive Summary, Technical Summary and the analysis of 47 domestic and international economic indicators are essential to executives who need to understand their economic environment and for the people responsible for planning for future trends. It is used by hundreds of business executives each month to keep them abreast of economic events, macroeconomic trends and specific financial and industry forecasts. All EcoTrends subscribers are invited to call an ITR analyst to discuss issues as they arise. We, in effect, become your 'in house' economists. In addition, all EcoTrends clients have access to our website's subscriber pages containing additional data trends and analysis of leading indicators that are updated within 24 hours of the release of the data.

Further, EcoTrends offers Economic Timing Analysis, which is "…a process in which we take your company's sales data history, convert it into a rate-of-change format, chart the data against U.S. industry and market indicators contained in EcoTrends, analyze the results and present you with your own company charts, giving you a view of the future. A follow-up phone consultation helps you understand the process and the implication of the results.

**National professional and industrial associations**: Your industry has a professional association that likely publishes regular newsletters, electronic news updates, monthly journals, and research reports. That association is likely headquartered in Washington, D.C. or Reston, Virginia where they maintain a legislative watchdog and lobbying staff. That association likely has an annual tradeshow and regional tradeshows. Make that association your association. Whatever the dues, they are worth it and will pay for themselves in one year. Put down the book and go on-line … and join.

# Appendix 2

## 10 changes that can increase the ROI of incentive/motivation programs

- Create a baseline set of measures from historical data of both revenue and expense, from the same time period as the proposed incentive program dates, with any one-time instances removed.

- Determine the incentive year baseline measures, for both revenue and expense, without consideration of the incentive program.

- Determine the incremental revenue and expense projections as a result of the incentive program, without consideration of the incentive program costs.

- Determine individual contribution of incremental revenue and expense for the incentive target audience to achieve overall incentive program projections.

- Determine the feasibility of individual effort to achieve the incremental incentive program revenue and expense projections.

- Determine the incentive award required to motivate the target audience to achieve the incentive revenue and expense projections.

- Calculate the incentive award investment required against the incremental net improvement of the incentive projections.

- Create a level playing field rules structure.

- Measure program results monthly; adjust rules to suit investment posture.

- Analyze final results for all incentive participants; take required action based on movement against objective for all, not just those who earned the award.

# Appendix 3

## 30 worst mistakes management makes with incentive/motivation programs

### Mistakes in Setting Objectives

- Set objectives that are based on what management wants to see, not what is realistic to achieve
- Set objectives without receiving input from departments that may be impacted by the incentive program activity
- Set objectives that are designed to create short term changes only
- Set objectives that conflict with other company goals and objectives

### Mistakes in Establishing Program Rules

- Establish rules that create that are not feasible for the entire incentive participant audience to achieve
- Establish rules that are not flexible over the life of the program
- Establish rules that are limited to financial aspects only
- Establish rules that are too hard to understand
- Establish rules that create havoc for other departments
- Establish rules without regard for individual/regional demographics
- Establish rules that create entitlement programs (80% repeat participants)

### Mistakes in Creating Incentive Budgets

- Create budgets based on what they think they can afford to spend
- Create budgets based on what they spent last year
- Create budgets without regard for incremental expenses from both incentive and non-incentive related departments
- Create budgets without forecasting incremental revenue from both incentive and non-incentive related departments
- Create budgets and truly believe they can negotiate better prices for the same value as a higher budget would cost
- Create budgets based on saving rather than investing

### Mistakes in Selecting Awards

- Select awards based on individual (buyer) feelings
- Select awards based on what their peers do
- Select awards without target audience demographic profiling
- Select awards based on price rather than perceived value
- Select awards based on distress or leverage pricing

## Mistakes in Program Measures

- Measure only high level financial results
- Measure only financial results
- Measure impact of incentive target group only
- Measure overall results only
- Don't measure any program results
- Don't establish measures at start of the program

## Mistakes in Program Participants

- Call the individuals who succeed "winners"
- Only pay attention to the "winners" at the conclusion of the program

# Appendix 4

## Dawson guide to incentive ROI terminology

If, after reading this book, you are truly ready to embark on creating an incentive program that demonstrates a true return on investment (ROI), these are terms you may want to review before you begin discussing this concept with your CFO or CEO.

### Terms NOT to use:

- Spiff
- Contest
- Drawing
- Trip
- Game
- Merch
- Awards
- Incentive
- Winners
- Win

Terms such as these will no doubt start you off on the wrong foot with your senior management team. Yes, even the word "incentive," which many perceive as perks to them, perks are trips, award merchandise, and even cash. To C Level executive, that spells E-X-P-E-N-S-E-S.

### Terms TO use:

- Investment
- Risk
- Return
- Return on Investment
- Earn
- Incremental
- Profits
- Cash Flow
- Stakeholder Value

These are terms your C level executives know and understand. This may be outside of your comfort zone, but I strongly urge you to go there.

# Appendix 5

## Maslow's Hierarchy of Needs applied with incentive programs

### Maslow's Hierarchy of Needs

Abraham Maslow developed a concept that has been widely recognized as one of the most sensible and credible explanations of what motivates people's actions and behaviors. Put simply, people climb to higher levels of need only when they satisfy more basic needs. The bottom of the hierarchy starts with physical sustenance and safety. Once that's satisfied, we all keep moving up the hierarchy. For incentive program managers, level 4 is important.

### Growth needs:

**Level 6 - Self-actualization**: "I'm satisfied. I strive only to build my character. "

**Level 5 - Aesthetic/cognitive needs**: "I strive for more knowledge, for a sense of order and balance in my life."

**Level 4 - Esteem needs**: "I need approval. I want recognition …*how am I doing?*"

### Basic deficiency needs:

**Level 3 - Belongingness/love needs:** 'I want acceptance, affiliation …*affection!*"

**Level 2 - Safety needs**: "I must be secure and safe! Where is my home?"

**Level 1 - Physiological needs**: "I am hungry. *Where is my next meal coming from?*"

# Appendix 6

## Return on investment (ROI) hierarchy of needs: Incentive buyer

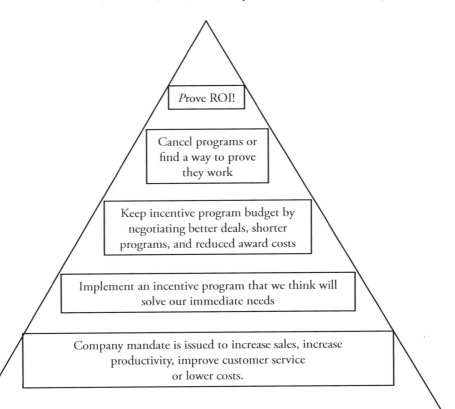

# Appendix 7

## Return on investment hierarchy of needs: Incentive participant

Job Hunting!

Incentive awards now seen as part of compensation

Begins to judge value of extra effort required to earn incentive awards with lower perceived value

Opportunity to earn high-perceived value incentive awards based on increased efforts; recognition by management, peer group, family, friends

Increased demands to do more with less; increased competitive forces; pressures to balance family/work life

# Appendix 8

## Peterson's 10 tests of a good market strategy

Strategy is a word we use in many ways, both in marketing and outside of our marketing lives ... if there is any such thing as time away from our marketing lives, right?

Here's the problem. In marketing, strategy has a vital role. Strategy is to marketing what the derivative and the limit are to the calculus. It is what double entries are to finance and accounting.

But it is commonplace to hear a CEO say, "Well, our strategy is to be the biggest widget maker in the Rocky Mountain region." That's more of an objective...and a very poorly stated one. Equally common is a top executive stating "Our strategy is to have ads in every trade journal." That's tactical, and probably not well integrated with other tactics.

How we position ourselves to be the top widget maker and the point we make in our ads is a creature of strategy. It's not unlike two officers on the bridge, one saying, "We're going this way" while the other asserts, "No, we should go that way." Sadly, top sales managers and marketers in the same company have similar disagreements. No wonder there is frequent conflict between sales and marketing leading to a ship that stops dead in the water.

To give strategic analysis the power it is due, ten guidelines are offered to identify the right direction for any enterprise, large or small. The goal is to use precise market strategy as the discipline behind all tactical decisions so that marketing programs flow logically and work efficiently.

1.  Your market strategy must reflect a competitive analysis that compares the relative strengths and weaknesses of each competitor and alternative to your offering.

2.  Your market strategy should be anchored to the unique added value you offer that survives your competitive analysis. (Also called unique selling proposition or USP). Not just *how* you are different, but *why* is that factor important to your target customers?

3.  Like a compass, your market strategy gives direction to your commercial voyage:

    ←   Where are we going?
    ←   Where don't we want to go?

4.  Your market strategy lends discipline to your objectives by answering the question "Ok, but how are you going to do all that?"

5.  Therefore, you can have only *one* market strategy per *product or target audience.* There is no such thing as "our market strategies are…" Also, a strategy statement should be limited to two sentences: one to showcase the uniqueness or added value of your offering and the second to proclaim how your offering benefits the customer.

6.  Your market strategy hangs on a clear, directional verb:

    •  "We will *focus* prospects' attention on our superior warranty."

    •  "Our strategy is *to concentrate* market attention on our overnight order fulfillment commitment"

    •  "We will *spotlight* the disadvantage of competitors' X factor and how we eliminate it"

    •  "We will *emphasize* our relationship (piggyback) with Acme Inc. to show added-value."

    •  "Our strategy is to *emphasize* that we bring our car repair service right to your office fleet."

7.  You cannot have a market strategy without consensus, from CEO to mailroom. Everyone must agree to it – including those who neither like it nor agree with it! (Intel has had remarkable success with consensus gained from every meeting they have).

8.  Considering steps 1 to 7, if you did not *agonize* over your market strategy, if you did not *think until it hurts*, you probably don't really have a good strategy. You can't do lunch to do strategy.

9.  And if your neighbor or your 12 year old can't understand your market strategy, it's not stated directly or simply enough for your employees and customers to "get it."

10. Lastly, if you can't create an advertising tagline (e.g. "Have It *Your* Way") that mirrors your strategy in seven or fewer neck grabbing words, go back to # 1.

3018039

Made in the USA